DISCOVERING
SAINT ANTHONY:
IF YOU ASK FOR MIRACLES

Prayers of a Catholic Community in Pittsburgh

DORETTA LONNETT WHALEN PHD, EDITOR

XULON PRESS

Xulon Press
2301 Lucien Way #415
Maitland, FL 32751
407.339.4217
www.xulonpress.com

Paperback ISBN-13: 978-1-6312-9445-7
Ebook ISBN-13: 978-1-6312-9446-4

DISCOVERING
SAINT ANTHONY:
IF YOU ASK FOR MIRACLES

December 3, 2022
Finalist

DEDICATION

Sincere gratitude to Rev. Robert J. Grecco,
Administrator of CGS Catholic Community.
Without your graciousness and positivity,
this book would not have been written.

CONTENTS

PART I: SIGNS AND WONDERS

PART II: ORAL HISTORY PROJECT

PART III: THE CHRISTMAS MESSAGE

FOREWORD

May God bless this book cover-to-cover.

PREFACE

I f you ask for miracles, you *can* receive them.

Recently, I had an unusual experience related to Saint Anthony—you could call it miraculous—and I felt I should share this broadly with others. But at the same time, I felt unworthy of dealing with this holy subject, and I was afraid of how it might be received. I devoted myself to praying for this intention, and surprisingly, I received a *further* sign! I was instantly supplied with the courage to go forward and it ignited in me a great desire to study Saint Anthony's life through reading and travel. I began to explore and pore over the materials available to me as a lay person, and I visited places where he walked, where his holiness is recognized.

Now the oral history project! I wanted to hear what faithful people might say about Saint Anthony's influence in their lives, so I constructed an oral history project to go among the parishioners in our Catholic community. And if this work hits home, it is because every single piece was given to me. Many voices express what is on their hearts— revealing stories running the gamut from heartbreaking to hilarious to modern-day miracles!

What emerges is an instrument with the restorative power of faith and the renewing resiliency of hope to ease the sense of fear, separation, and loss prevalent in our world. As the cruel Coronavirus-19 threatens to take charge, and in the face of every discouraging issue in our lives, I hope this book lifts you up as you join me in discovering Saint Anthony.

Special thanks to the following former SSJ pastors whose example encouraged constant prayer:
Rev. John (Jay) Donahue.
Rev. Daniel J. Maurer, S.T.L.
Rev. Richard E. Ward, S.T.D.

I am grateful to all parishioners in our CGS Catholic community:
Saint Elizabeth Ann Seton (SEAS) in Carnegie.
Saint Margaret of Scotland (SMOS) in Green Tree.
Saints Simon and Jude (SSJ) in Scott Township.
Thank you for your words of encouragement, for sharing your stories, and for your continuing prayers.

In addition, I would like to acknowledge the following:

Margaret Behrens, for book info.

David Convertino, O.F.M.: Executive Director of HNP Office of Development,

for permission to print prayer cards.

Green Tree Public Library staff.

Dave Grinnell of Historic Pittsburgh.

Maria Hart: Director of Anthonian Assn., Chicago.

Mark Jackovic: Education & Archives Manager, Manchester Craftsmen's Guild.

Louise Marino, for photo of St. Anthony plaque.

Helen and Ramesh Ohol, for Christmas photos.

Saints Simon and Jude Church office staff.

Rev. Aleksandr J. Schrenk, for help in editing notes content.

Mary Kay Smith, for CGS Parish Bulletin ad designs.

Judy Tammaro, for Foreword blessing, and for "looking forward" to the movie.

Marilyn Teolis, for editing front and back content.

Mt. Lebanon Public Library.

Denise Thomas: Office Manager of *The Pitt News*.

Danielle Sarta: Pre-Production Representative, Salem Author Services (Xulon Press).

Alexandria Zaldivar: Production Representative, Salem Author Services (Xulon Press).

LIST OF ABBREVIATIONS

ACCESS	Allegheny County Coordinated Effort for Shared-ride Services.
APR	American Public Radio.
CGS	Carnegie, Green Tree and Scott.
C.PP.S.	Missionaries of the Precious Blood.
ER	Emergency Room.
EWTN	Eternal Word Television Network.
FR.	Father.
GPS	Global Positioning System.
HNP	Holy Name Province.
IX	Nine or ninth in Roman numerals (I=-1, X=10).
LIII	53 in Roman numerals (L=50, I=1).
MCG	Manchester Craftsmen's Guild.

MIC	Marian Fathers of the Immaculate Conception.
NAB	The New American Bible.
O.F.M.	Order of Friars Minor.
O.F.M. Cap.	Order of Friars Minor, Capuchin.
O.F.M. Conv.	Order of Friars Minor, Conventual.
O.F.S.	Order of Secular Franciscans.
O.P.	Order of Preachers; Dominicans.
PCP	Primary Care Physician.
REV.	Reverend.
S.A.	Servant of God, Apostle of Christian Unity and Charity.
SEAS	Saint Elizabeth Ann Seton Catholic Church.
SJ	Society of Jesus; Jesuits.
SMOS	Saint Margaret of Scotland Catholic Church.
SS.	Saints.
SSJ	Saints Simon and Jude Catholic Church.
S.T.D.	Doctor of Sacred Theology.
S.T.L.	Licentiate of Sacred Theology.
T.A.	Teaching Assistant.

Introduction

METHODS

T his book is divided into three parts utilizing different approaches. As a college lecturer, I sought to develop ways to engage my students while taking into account varied learning styles and levels of experience, and the same applies with readership.

What follows is a brief explanation of each part and feature in this book.

PART I: SIGNS AND WONDERS

I share how I came to write this book with personal stories and disclosing some unusual experiences related to Saint Anthony as well as my growth process through prayer.

PART II: ORAL HISTORY PROJECT

The goal was to acquire responses from 60 members of the Catholic community to which I belong, specifically individuals who could answer "yes" to the leading question: "Have you ever lost something and then prayed to St. Anthony?"

An ad in the parish bulletin got the word out. I supplemented a poster placed in strategic spots when church activities drew a crowd, such as SMOS' Cash Bash and SEAS' pancake breakfast. The poster displayed the leading question, the bulletin ad, and tear-offs with my contact information. The final count exceeded expectations and includes six persons who are either immediate family or friends of parishioners or persons who sometimes attend our masses and church functions.

You will find amusement in the Lost and Found Pictorial Index. Some of the lost items are pictured, and readers may wish to "find" these items, matching them with the storyteller and their story.

MIRACLES

My inspiration for organization of the stories comes from an early source.

After Anthony's funeral in 1231, there were reports of many miracles at his tomb and elsewhere. These are contained in the book, *Assidua*.

"*Assidua* or *Vita Prima* is the earliest writing on Anthony.It was written in Latin, the official language of the church during this time and for hundreds of years henceforth. *Assidua* was written by a Franciscan friar who was Saint Anthony's contemporary. We don't know the author's name, but it is known that he wrote this "First Life" by mandate of his Paduan superior and at the request of his confreres, completing it in 1232."[1]

The medieval author includes a collection of fifty-three (LIII) miracles in the chapter, "Here Begin the Miracles of Blessed Anthony," which were compiled and read "in the presence of the Lord Pope Gregory (IX) and in the listening of all the people."[2]

He grouped them by category. For example, "The Physically Disabled" contains nineteen stories. There are seven stories about "The Blind." And there are singular accounts as well, such as "The Unbroken Drinking Glass."

In this book, I have chosen to categorize the stories according to thirteen themes. Some stories seem to defy classification since they touch on several themes, but at this point, I like where they live.

Sometimes material in stories lends itself to explanation and/or further discussion. These points are marked with superscripts, leading the reader, sooner or later, to Notes that flesh out items of interest and of historical importance — not only of Saint Anthony of Padua but also of the Franciscan Order he joined and of its founder, Saint Francis of Assisi. However, it is not necessary to read the Notes in order to understand and thoroughly enjoy the stories.

PART III: A CHRISTMAS MESSAGE

Each of the churches in our community has a unique identity, and our people take pride in their home churches. There is perhaps no better representation of this than photographs of their nativity scenes.

Part I:

SIGNS AND WONDERS

MY TESTIMONY

A friend just reminded me that falling down is a part of life, but the important thing is getting back up and living. I married young and didn't have the inner strength to cope well with my new role as wife and mother as well as working full-time. I wish I had possessed the wisdom to make better decisions. Despite counseling, my marriage ended.

It is still painful to revisit this, but it was a significant part of my life. I want to share so you know I received consolation and strength and healing in the blessed sacraments of the Catholic faith. I met Gene, a man who invited me to mass at SSJ, and this is where we were married in 1997. In this environment, I found a very fulfilling spiritual life, serving God in serving the wonderful people of this community.

My daughters and I often share good reads, and at one point, Sonya gave me *33 Days to Morning Glory* by Fr. Michael E. Gaitley.[3] I completed the Do-It-Yourself Retreat program on July 16, 2016, the date of my consecration to the Blessed Virgin Mary. Reciting aloud the daily Act of Consecration I composed from various parts of that text has given my life even more direction. First thing every morning, I ask the Lord "to make me a pure heart."

This fortification had arrived just in time. My mother died five weeks after my consecration. My daughter suggested I share my morning offering:

> "Driven with passion to make me a pure heart, in union with the most Immaculate Heart of Mary, I consecrate my life to the Mother of Christ, whom Jesus entrusted to me, and I to her, as He died on the cross. I accept as my duty all that happens in this day as coming from her, for she is the creature who glorifies God most perfectly. I trust that she will share with me her virtues and purify me and my actions, so that I may grow closer and closer to Jesus, who suffered beyond all suffering for my sins and those of the whole world."

A few months after Mother died, our church offered a workshop on another of Father Gaitley's retreats, *Consoling the Heart of Jesus*.[4]Because I had received great benefit from his self-help program, I enrolled, hoping this interactive format might be more helpful to me as I was moving through feelings of loss. Heidi Potter and Bethann Petrovich were excellent facilitators, and everyone there had such a loving heart for the Lord and each other. I consecrated on May 15, 2017. Again, this action proved to be fortifying since Gene and I would learn of his terminal illness a month or so later. Here is my "self-composed" Act of Consecration from choice phrases in Gaitley's text:

"Dearest Merciful Father,
My self-confidence has been replaced with complete and utter confidence in You, for You said that Your power is made more perfect in weakness. In the name of our lovable Jesus, the Virgin Mary and all the saints, I ask that You set me on fire with Your spirit of love. Make me a victim of Your love, allowing the waves of infinite tenderness of Your Divine Mercy to overflow into my soul, so that I might do little things with great love, and so that You may be more deeply loved in this imperfect world. This I ask in Jesus' name. Amen."

Gene passed on October 23, 2017, leaving me in a sad place, but I did not become depressed. Instead, I clung to Jesus, Mary, and my family and true friends here.

The most recent step I've taken to increase my spirituality was through visiting a Marian shrine. Sonya and I went on pilgrimage to Mexico City in May 2019, to the Basilica of Our Lady of Guadalupe.[5] It was a prayerful experience for us with daily Mass in several churches, each one more awe-inspiring than the previous.

But what touched me most was that Our Lady chose the humble setting of Tepeyac Hill for her appearance. She spoke to a native Indian, and she chose flowers as a sign. This occurred nearly 500 years ago, but her message is fresh, and I returned home with the desire to decode it fully and with the challenge to live this love more and more and more.

THE EARRING QUERY

FEBRUARY 2018

Three months after Gene died, my neighbor's mother passed away. John had lovingly cared for his mother at home for several years, so I had gotten to know her. I knew what it was to lose your mother because, as I've shared, my mother had passed in August, 2016. I was still mourning the loss of both her and my husband. I didn't fear slipping into depression, though, as I had very attentive family and friends and a strong prayer life.

John invited me and another friend to ride along with him to the out-of-town service where we visited at the funeral home, the grave site, and then we had lunch at a restaurant with his relatives before driving back to Pittsburgh. The weather was very mild for February, and now I cannot recall what I wore, except for my favorite earrings I'd bought for a song from an indoor vendor at Trader Jack's some years ago.

It was Gene who had introduced me to Trader Jack's. We would stroll those lanes after Sunday mass—a treasure hunt for me—but not his favorite thing. He broke it to me gently after one sweltering Sunday morning when we were dressed to the nines and suffering. I will correct myself here to give Gene a ten; I was a six at best. He was a superlative artist and designer who had created logos for Fortune 500 companies, and this was just one niche of the art industry in which he excelled.

After that day in the sun, when Sunday rolled around, Gene would tear out a bill from his wallet and wave me off with a smile. This was his blessing for an adventure that I fully embraced. Twenty dollars at a flea market can buy an *awful* lot, and sometimes I did.

As a child of the sixties, I had a thing for vintage jewelry, and Trader Jack's had this one pair of earrings that were pretty, pastel pink and yellow, and just my style. Though plastic may not be the epitome of sophistication, they were unique, and certainly irreplaceable.

But somehow, on the day I attended the funeral the unthinkable had happened! I didn't realize it until that evening, when I was getting ready for bed, that one was missing!

I started into the lost earring routine. If *you* wear earrings, it may be *your* Plan A, and it's happened so often that I've composed a little poem for it:

Check the floor...maybe it fell.
Check your hair...maybe it's there.
Check your clothing...maybe it's clinging.

If that fails, I move on to Plan B: Retrace my steps.

But before leaving the bedroom on this night, I knelt and prayed to Saint Anthony:

"Dear Saint Anthony, help me find what I have lost, my earring, and I will pray.

Dear Saint Anthony, help me find what I have lost, my earring, and I will pray.
Dear Saint Anthony, help me find what I have lost, my earring, and I will pray."

Then I prayed Our Father, Hail Mary, and Glory Be. After paying Saint Anthony due respect I continued the search. But I admit that it can be an exercise in patience to do the praying this way when I am most anxious to apply my energies to the hunt.

I stepped down the hardwood stairs, moving my head like a typewriter carriage trying not to miss any area on the stairs, then onto the rug, and out onto the porch. It was already dark, but the area outside my condo is very well lit, and this large, colorful piece would not escape my lost jewelry radar. I retraced my steps around the building and down the wide cement walk to the street.

What I didn't mention is that Tuesday February 13, 2018 was an unusually eventful day. After returning with John from the funeral and wake for his mother, I don't remember how I passed the couple hours at home until my trusted, talented T.A. Irene and her optimistic, thoughtful mother Susie arrived to give me a lift. They pulled up to my front steps, and then we were off to the Manchester Craftsmen's Guild Concert Hall on the North Side.

At the time, I was teaching History of Jazz at the University of Pittsburgh and had received an invitation to attend the premiere of the film documentary, *We Knew What We Had: The Greatest Jazz Story Never Told.*[6] My mentor at Pitt, ethnomusicologist, jazz saxophonist, and educator Dr. Nathan Davis, was one of the spokespersons in the film. He left teaching early in the decade and officially retired in 2013. I hadn't seen him since, but I called him later that week to congratulate him and to wish him a happy birthday. It was the last time we chatted. He passed away in April.

Susie drove into the MCG lot, nearly full, so we had to park far from the door. The film was sensational! A reception followed, and we used the restrooms. This means the earring could have fallen in any of these places or, of course, at the events in the morning. Or, maybe it was in Susie's car.

At home that evening, after combing the sidewalk, I called Susie. She and Irene checked the car right away but didn't find the earring. So I searched throughout my place.

Instead of my going into detail about the next few days, suffice it to say that I made a barrage of phone calls, and I conducted daily inspections of the sidewalk. John wanted to donate his mother's hospital bed, so he and our kind-hearted friend Steve dragged that along the walk and down the front steps to his vehicle.

On Wednesday of the following week, Irene offered me a ride home from campus. Typically, I rode the bus *to* Pitt for the Monday and Wednesday lecture classes. On those days I would leave through my back door and walk down the hill to the bus stop. Irene usually drove to campus though, and when she didn't have a class conflict after the lecture, she might offer me a ride home. I hemmed and hawed until she insisted, "Come on!"

During the ride home we covered the usual topics, and then the talk came around to my earring. I was saying how I would *love* to find it. I'd worn them with Gene to dinners, and I considered them a gift from him—even though I picked them out—because he had paid for them.

Pulling up to my house, she did a U-turn so I could exit her car close to the curb and the front steps. I opened the car door, and there was my earring!!! It was on the sidewalk just a few inches from the curb!!

It was uncanny to find this now, a week later, in a place I had looked many times. And to think it was in view right in the center of the sidewalk, right where her car was stopped, like it was placed there, for me, waiting to be discovered! Irene and I looked at each other, shivering. To think too, that had I taken the bus home that day, I would not have seen it!

Later, as I reflected on that moment, I realized I had prayed fervently to Saint Anthony from the start and throughout the week, as I shamelessly desired to reclaim this "I-can't-lose-this-too" object. It was such a sad time for me, that when the earring was returned to me, I was overjoyed!

"But *how* do you explain the return of the earring? How do I explain this?" I spread the good news to my daughters, sisters, etc. Nearly everyone told me my husband was "up there!" or "right here!" or things like "That's Gene!" and "Gene is looking out for you!"

I truly wondered whether it was Gene who had done this. He had passed away just four months prior. Was he still with me as well-wishers were saying? And did he have the power to move objects? Maybe he could see my pain and wanted to help me. I *wanted* to believe it all. Or, do I need to thank Saint Anthony for the surprising return of my earring? Who *was* responsible? This was on my mind.

Just a couple of days passed, and knowing that my gas gauge was close to E, I planned to fill up the tank and go to the grocery store.

In my car I kept three religious objects in view: a green plastic rosary hanging on the rear view mirror reminding me of my mother, a chaplet rosary given to me by *mi querida amiga* (my dear friend) Celmira in the center storage space under the dashboard panel, and my Sacred Heart Auto League cross. I had that taped onto the glove compartment for years.

I touched the beads lightly and backed out of my garage, and once on the common road I coasted down the hill and pulled into GetGo. At the gas station I went through all the motions we do when pumping gas and using a credit card. And then, closing the gas cap hatch, I opened the car door to get back in and get going but saw something that made me say, "What is *that*??" I must have said it aloud!

There was a small, shiny gold disc on my navy seat cushion. It certainly wasn't there when I got out of the car, and it wasn't there when I'd gotten in. I picked it up to examine it and saw some letters and a figure, but there was a car behind me wanting to move, so I pulled out and returned home.

The object wasn't familiar to me at all, and I was trying to figure out where in the world it came from. This was strange, and I was very curious to see the details. I immediately grabbed the magnifying glass and could now see clearly, "ST ANTHONY PRAY FOR US."

I was trembling. I have *never* owned or carried or worn a Saint Anthony medal. I do have several medals of the Blessed Mother which I wear and keep on my dresser. My father was named Anthony, and neither had I known him to have one. I examined the piece very closely. It is imprinted on just one side. It's thinner than a dime with a circumference of 13/16".

The embossed image is The Saint, his right arm around baby Jesus who is sitting on a book. The Saint is holding a lily in his left hand. There are rays leading out from him to the lettering around the edge. You can see this find on this book's back cover and on the Epigraph.

THE SIGN

THURSDAY OCTOBER 17, 2019

It seemed like an ordinary autumn day in Pittsburgh—chilly, even gloomy—as gray skies promised a visitation of showers. Despite the attractiveness of remaining in my cozy condo, I had an early afternoon appointment scheduled with a new podiatrist—at least she was new to me. My PCP had recommended her at my annual wellness visit.

I wanted to know whether the young doctor might have any new methods of care for problem feet. And when I telephoned for an appointment, I learned she was already well established, with four offices including one in the South Hills where I live. The receptionist asked which location I wanted, and for some reason I said, "Shadyside!" I had retired from Pitt in the summer of 2018, so I would enjoy the two-bus jaunt through town and my old stomping grounds.

On the appointed day, I packed a number of essentials into my waterproof shoulder bag and drove to the Park and Ride, just a piece up the road, to catch the bus to downtown.

Finding a front seat, I settled back to compose my thoughts, trying to settle what was *really* on my mind. Every blessed morning now, for at least two weeks, I awakened brimming with ideas for a formidable writing project in a religious vein. But why me? With my children living in other parts of the country, I feel I'm coming to terms with my life of solitude. And at the same time, I already have *plenty* of activities to keep me as busy and as challenged as I wish to be at this stage in my life, and this includes some volunteer work. And I have four grandchildren I'd like to see more often.

So, here's the thing: I need to stop making excuses and face this. I feel that I am being *called* to do this project.

> "God, if you are truly calling me, then I need a sure sign—something I cannot miss—something unmistakable. I believe you have already made it clear to me that Saint Anthony's gifts are real. And I believe this wholeheartedly. If I am going to throw myself full force into work that will honor Saint Anthony and worship You, whom he worships, then I am asking for a *further* sign."

It was just before noon when the second bus delivered me to the Shadyside Medical Center where I had my miserable feet photographed, and then I went up to Dr. Sciulli's office. She was wonderful, sharing the latest products to help make walking (and tap dancing) more comfortable.

I was smiling as I left her third-floor office, taking the elevator back down and stepping out into the wide corridor. I could hear my footsteps ring on the tiles as I proceeded into the lobby with its wall of windows. A gentle rain glanced along the panes in panorama.

Pausing a few feet before the door to pull the umbrella from my bag, I turned my head to a voice resonating from the back of the busy lobby. A thin African-American gentleman stood tall, seeming to hold court with those standing with him. He had a smile in his voice as he proclaimed: "My name is Anthony! Italians call me Antonio! The French call me Antoine!"

I popped my umbrella open, and just before exiting I called to him, "Ciao, Antonio!"

Somewhat surprised, he looked in my direction, smiled broadly, and waved.

Joyfully, I stepped up and down the driveway curb, recalling Gene Kelly's *Singing in the Rain.*[7] The bus was already in view, and when I settled in my seat, it hit me! This was the sign! The subject of my project is Saint *Anthony.* I had by that time read enough to know that Anthony had a *strong voice* that could *project loudly* and *clearly.* And he was a *popular* figure, and that people flocked to hear him preach.

I wondered at the scene that had taken place in just seconds in that busy lobby. The time, the place, the circumstances, sight and sound, and even the weather converged to answer my prayer. The sequence played over and over, the details burned into my mind. I could never forget. And in days to come, I found this event to be even more significant! With further reading, I learned that Anthony *had* preached in southern France. So he *was* called Antoine.

This sealed the deal! I was anxious to get started. And in the weeks that followed, I would receive two more signs that were unexpected and unusual.

HE KNOWS OUR NEEDS

WEDNESDAY NOVEMBER 27, 2019

Immediately following the 8:30 a.m. mass on Wednesday, the day before Thanksgiving, I walked into the SSJ social hall to attend today's class. Father Alek was offering a course on *Confessions* by St. Augustine.[8] I really wanted to attend, since Saint Anthony's foundation was Augustinian. I knew Father's talks would provide insight. I perched my homemade sign on the music stand in a place where I guessed it would be seen—near the coffee and munchies.

Then I settled in a seat at one of the round tables, prepared to take notes. I noticed a parishioner across the room whom I'd run into last Wednesday at morning mass. She is a Eucharistic minister, and she told me she'd meet me in a week to provide an interview. Today was Wednesday again. Since I hadn't heard from her, I thought she'd forgotten. But there she was standing beside me, pulling on her gloves.

"Listen I've gotta run. Why don't you come with me?"

"What?"

"We can talk in my car!"

She told me a little about Saint Anthony and a lot about her life story in the faith. All the while my phone recorder is picking up her words, her delightful inflections and so on. It was inspiring to hear her testimony, but I wondered how much would be pertinent to the book. My focus was Saint Anthony. But she was so kind to embrace the cause. Of course I was drawn in by her enthusiasm, and I so appreciated her support for this project.

She turned off the main road into the parking lot of a nursing home. This was unexpected. When she said she was going to a _home_, I understood that to mean a house. I told her I'd be happy to wait in the car, but she said, "No, come in. I want you to meet 'my people.'"

She introduced me right off, but still I felt a bit out of place as my bubbly friend conversed with the resident, a sweet woman who was obviously happy to see her. The two spent several minutes together in prayer, and then my friend gave her Holy Communion and wished her a happy Thanksgiving.

I thought to myself, "What a caring person she is to give her time in this way, to bless these people who have visitors so infrequently." As we headed down the hallway, I was becoming a bit impatient, though, because I kept thinking I needed time to be on task. I'd set a goal for sixty respondents. Her story took me to twenty. "Oh," I thought, "I still have quite a way to go, and this time away isn't doing me any good."

I wished that I could go back to the social hall where there were several people in the class, and maybe one of them might grant me an interview afterward. Besides that, I'd just booked European trip, squeezed in just before Christmas. So all of this was on my mind. Then I felt her pulling on the arm of my jacket.

"Come on," she said, gently tugging my sleeve. "We're going into lockdown hall now."

We stepped on, then off the elevator, and there was a guard seated at the desk. My friend signed us in.

I could feel a lump in my throat as we walked into a dim room where a woman was quite still in her chair facing the window, the bright light shining on her face and hair. It seemed to me that she might be much less responsive than the woman we'd just visited.

My friend broke the silence: "I'd like you to meet Doretta. She is a cantor from church who is writing a book on Saint Anthony."

The woman's voice was thin but surprisingly spirited. "I *love* Saint Anthony! I was *named* for Saint Anthony. I was born on his feast day, June thirteenth."

This was startling! I could tell that it was *news* to my friend. She and I exchanged glances, and I wondered if she was thinking what I was: This woman must be confused because her name was not in any way a derivative of "Anthony."

"What was the last thing you remember Saint Anthony doing for you?" she asked her, and, "Did you lose anything and pray to Saint Anthony?" It made me smile to hear my friend using the techniques I'd fashioned for this probe and to realize she was so familiar with the leading question.

The woman answered softly, "I don't remember now, I can't remember so far back."

"What was the last thing that you lost, and did you find it?"

"Yes, I did," the woman answered. "I can't remember, though. I pray to him for lost things. I have a little prayer book, a little leaflet, like, with all the prayers to Saint Anthony. I say that *all* the time."

My friend told her she would bring her a book about Saint Anthony the next time. The woman beamed at her, and then my friend told her that maybe I'd sing a song at communion. The woman looked at me and smiled.

So I mentally rehearsed the words of a song I thought would be meaningful, and at the appropriate moment, I was somehow able to get out one verse of "Jesus, My Lord, My God, My All." Then my friend bid her good-bye and wished her a happy Thanksgiving. She walked past me toward the door, but I quickly stepped over to the woman's chair.

"Is your middle name Antonia?"

"No. Antoinette!!"

I was reassured and felt energized and blessed by what had happened there. And I knew that even as the work of this project would become more challenging, I would not be abandoned.

THE POWER OF PRAYER

DECEMBER 2019–JANUARY 2020

The oral history project was well underway. I was super-charged and excited to travel to places where The Saint had lived. While the Italian connection is evident in The Saint's title, "Saint Anthony of Padua," it may be surprising to learn that he was Portuguese. Born in Lisbon during the last decade of the twelfth century, he was called Ferdinand/Fernando (cf. Note 22.p.158 and Note 36. p.166). He pursued a path of holiness which propelled him on an astonishing trajectory–from the Augustinian monastery to the newly-formed Franciscan Order–journeying in Italy and France, teaching and preaching the Word of God, and leaving for posterity a treasury of Gospel commentaries.

I followed through with my plans, and my European trip was a dream! Tour guides Pedro and Deborah, whom I'd discovered online, were phenomenal! The Basilica di Sant'Antonio di Padova was beyond description![9] In the gift shop there, I purchased a few primary sources that were difficult to get hold of in the U.S. This made my bag much heavier coming home (Lufthansa checked my overweight bag at no cost).

Thank God I traveled from December 15–22. If I had waited for better weather, it may not have happened at all, for the pandemic has caused flights to Italy to be cancelled, and the Basilica is in lockdown. When I was making plans to go, my daughters could not understand their mother doing such a thing, especially since I had been inward, sad, and somewhat fearful in the previous months, following the deaths of my mother and husband. But I had found peace through prayer, and I had a fire in me for this mission.

When I arrived home, I didn't get around to reading the new volumes right away because I was hungry for interviews to take place before my self-imposed deadline of February 28. When I left the U.S., the number of respondents was thirty-two, just over halfway to the goal. Now, in the week following Christmas, I had to step up the pace.

It was mid-January when I got to the thinnest book with this passage:

> "Father Joseph Abate has discovered a sermon in a thirteenth century manuscript which is ascribed to the hand of one of Saint Anthony's confreres. It tells of a previously unknown episode of a very distinctly Franciscan flavour, a real "little flower" in the life of the Wonder-Worker. On 2nd February, perhaps of 1231, the day of the Purification of St. Mary, founded and dedicated to the Virgin by himself, the Saint was singing a responsory in his lovely voice: "Obtulerunt pro eo Domino par turturum aut duos pullos columbarum..." (They offered to the Lord for the return of Jesus two turtle doves or two pigeons).He wanted to know exactly what the Poor Virgin had offered for the return of her Son, whether

it was two turtle doves or two pigeons…and two turtle doves flew over the pulpit where Anthony was singing!" We think of his joy and of the astonishment of those present. With ingenuous tenderness, Mary had revealed the gift she had made in the Temple: a couple of turtle doves."[10]

Gamboso comments, "He who had so loved Mary, and brought so many others to love her…Anthony's doctrinal contributions…affirmed with certainty that the divine Redeemer glorified his beloved Mother, from whom he had taken human flesh, to the highest degree."[11]

Anthony was educated, and he highly valued knowledge of Scripture. According to the above account as given by Father Abate, Anthony had an honest question about an event that had taken place over a thousand years before his time; the answer was not in any record. Yet he received an immediate answer, witnessed by many.

I was struck by this amazing story. Despite being unworthy of receiving such a gift, I saw a connection with what I had experienced in finding the Saint Anthony token, which I believe was the answer to *my* question as to whom was responsible for the unusual appearance of the lost earring. And I feel graced and blessed by all of these experiences.

The Power of Prayer: "Ask, and you will receive. Seek, and you will find. Knock, and it will be opened to you. For the one who asks, receives. The one who seeks, finds."[12]

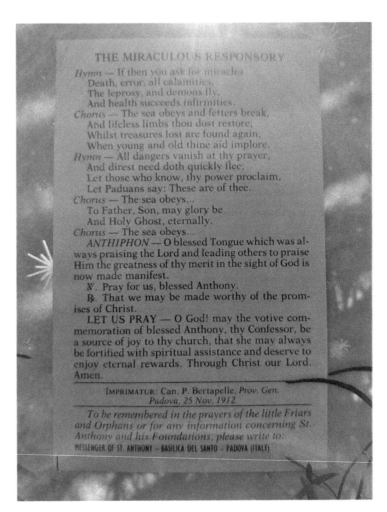

Figure 1.

Part II:

ORAL HISTORY PROJECT

FROM THE CHAPEL
ON THE HILL

FR. ALEK SCHRENK

The prayer that I was taught as a child is "Saint Anthony, Saint Anthony, come around. Something's lost and must be found." It's sort of a children's rhyme, so I don't typically pray that whenever I need the intercession of Saint Anthony, though it often comes to mind!It was probably one of my parents who taught it to me. My mother didn't grow up Catholic, so it wouldn't have been something she knew as a child, but I think she was the one who taught it to me. Typically, though, my prayers to Saint Anthony are much more direct. I feel like I've known him for many, many years so I can address him in normal terms.

My dad's family is from Troy Hill where Saint Anthony's Chapel is located.[13] Our family is of German extraction, and my great-great-grandfather built a house there which is still in the family. When he was a child he knew Father Suitbert Mollinger, the priest who commenced the building of the chapel in 1880. So my family has some interesting memories of those times.

In the 1970s, the chapel was falling into disrepair, but the people of the parish rallied on their own to preserve the chapel. They came together to raise money and did a lot of the work to make that happen. And so my great-grandfather was one of the early chapel sitters. He and other volunteers would sit in the chapel certain hours during the day so that it could be kept open. This happened before I was born, but it is one of the stories I've heard.

I have many of my own memories of going to Saint Anthony's Chapel as a boy, for example, going to the novena on Tuesdays with my dad. And I recall many other family experiences from Saint Anthony's. So there has always been for me and my family a very strong connection to Saint Anthony's Chapel. And of all the saints I would consider to be patrons of mine, Saint Anthony is very high up there.

I always keep with me a holy card of Saint Anthony. My wallet is very minimal. I have my Giant Eagle Advantage card (as everyone does!), my driver's license, some insurance information, the old mission statement when I was a student at Duquesne University—and they tell you to keep that with you, and I did—but I keep his holy card with me as well.

When I was ordained a priest, I had this card commissioned. And so there are four saints I chose for the border. First, St. Damasus, a pope whose feast day is on my birthday. I chose him as my Confirmation saint. Then there's Saint Paul, for the Diocese of Pittsburgh, and Saint John the Baptist, because I was ordained on the Feast of the Nativity of Saint John the Baptist. And, of course, one of them is Saint Anthony with the lily and the Christ child, because of the connection I have…because Saint Anthony is very special to me.

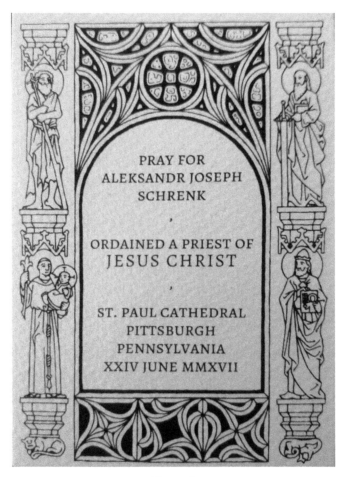

PRAY FOR
ALEKSANDR JOSEPH
SCHRENK

,

ORDAINED A PRIEST OF
JESUS CHRIST

,

ST. PAUL CATHEDRAL
PITTSBURGH
PENNSYLVANIA
XXIV JUNE MMXVII

Figure 2.

THE LIGHT OF FAITH

"There are many people who profit from our little light of faith."
~ Fr. Jerome Etenduk, (Homily, Feb 13 2020) ~

GRACE

I pray to Saint Anthony when I lose things:
"Saint Anthony dressed in brown,[14]
I've lost something and it must be found."

PAT

My personality is, I lose things all the time.

It happens almost daily or every other day, so as soon as I can't find something, I say,

"Saint Anthony, in Jesus' name, *please* help me find this."

And the prayer is just simply my talking to God and asking for a saint's intercession.

So often I'll just turn around or look somewhere, and it is there. It isn't always the case, but I would say it is a great deal of the time.

I think Saint Anthony has more gifts than just finding things, and I sometimes feel guilty that this is often my prayer request, to find things. It just seems trite in some ways.

Yes, I think he has a lot more spiritual gifts. I ask him to help me in my knowledge of scripture too. I believe that was one of his strengths.

DEACON JIM

My wife and I were talking last night, and she was wondering, did we ever think of praying to Saint Anthony for lost souls, for somebody that's gone astray, somebody that needs found, that needs to be brought back to God?

Maybe Saint Anthony gets bored looking for keys, cell phones and wedding rings. Maybe a meaningful use of his intercession—a very meaningful use—would be to pray for lost souls. There are plenty of them around. And it would be good to put him to work doing that.

ANONYMOUS PARISHIONER

This happened just three days ago, and I want everyone to know that Saint Anthony *never* fails me, and he is good for much more important matters than finding things like car keys.

My teenage daughter ran away from home. I was beside myself and drove around searching for her. I carried her photo to places, asking, "Have you seen this girl? If you do, *please* call this number!"

And while I searched, I prayed, "Through the intercession of Saint Anthony, let me find my daughter."

The police found her, unharmed.

SHARON

A few years ago, I posted on Facebook a story of lost and found—found thanks to Saint Anthony.

A couple years after my mom had passed away, my daughter was graduating from high school, and in order to feel close to her grandma, she was wearing Grandma's watch that was given to her. She kept the watch on throughout the time of graduation because she missed Grandma so much at this pivotal point in her life. On the day of her graduation party the weather was beautiful, so she and her friends spent a lot of time outside. She had been with her friends in the yard, throughout the house and the neighbor's yard where they played games.

Later in the day, my daughter had come to me in distress and crying that she had lost Grandma's watch. I was troubled because this token of Grandma was one that kept my daughter feeling connected with my mom. Being upset for my daughter and wanting to comfort her, I said to her, "Well, let's pray to Saint Anthony first and foremost because we know the watch is *here*. He will help us find it!"

We stopped and prayed together.

Saint Anthony is so special to me. He has helped my family in many ways. He has helped me, through prayer, with the illnesses of my kids, and of course with lost items.

What a moment! The beauty was that everybody had stopped what they were doing and joined us. Everybody was praying with us. They all were concerned and wanted this child to find this piece which was a link to her grandmother with whom she had been so close. Then we searched, and we searched, and about twenty minutes later the watch was found, way in the neighbor's yard where they had been playing kickball. *That's* what they were doing!

But I will always remember the beautiful example and witness of faith, to see everyone at the party praying together—some who knew Saint Anthony well and others who were introduced to him that day.

NANCY

My father was from Ireland. My mother was German and French. And our family may be relatives of the Little Flower, and they are researching that. But I learned about praying to Saint Anthony through our grandparents, who were deeply devoted Catholics. So, I just knew as a child to say a prayer if I lost something.

One of my dear friends who passed away from cancer a few years ago would say the rhyme all the time. Do you know that rhyme? Anyway, after you've found what was missing, you put money in the collection for the poor. So I *do* that, because I think, "Well, this will help somebody else."

My life is a continual prayer to Saint Anthony. I don't say the little rhyme. I just say something simple like, "Please Saint Anthony, help me," or, "Dear Saint Anthony, I just can't find this. Could you help me?"

They are usually common things like jewelry, credit cards, purses, glasses—common things, everyday things. And honestly, probably within *the* hour, I find it, or I come across it. What's really unusual is that in some cases, I have already looked in *that* spot and didn't see it before.

Yes, as I said, it's either the keys or a credit card that fell somewhere, and I looked in that place before, and it wasn't there. But then after I say the prayer, it just appears there.

It would have been around the year 2000, I was having some work done at my house, putting on an addition. There's a *lot* of work and renovation in these old houses. And I also bought a statue of Saint Anthony for my garden then.

Anyway, it was during this same time that I was missing my wedding ring. It was missing for a *long* time. I said a prayer to Saint Anthony. And it took *time*, but it was found. And guess where it was? It was between the wall covering and the wall! It was glued onto the (laugh) wallpaper glue! This was discovered *after* the work was finished in the bathroom. I noticed a lump in the paper near the baseboard, and I wondered what it was? I ripped the strip of wallcovering up and away from the wall, and *there* was my wedding ring! It was very strange. I couldn't figure out how it got there??

PATRICIA

Saint Anthony is my main man! Oh my heavens, that's how we started, since I was a kid, but I pray to him daily, and he has done so much for me.

As a matter of fact, as soon as I get in the car, he's my co-pilot. Just the other day on Greentree Road, I was almost in a collision, and I believe Saint Anthony interceded and stopped the other car!

My husband was German. His family came from Germany. I'm German/Irish. But, when my husband was gravely ill, I prayed that he wouldn't suffer. And my prayer was answered. He passed away peacefully. It will be three years this month.

You know, I have grandchildren. My granddaughter and grandson are in college, and though I keep in close touch, I don't know everything that goes on with them, but I always ask Saint Anthony to protect them and guide them to excel. My grandson is really keeping up with his grades, and his sister had an A average when she finished her junior year.

My faith was tested this past December 28th when my granddaughter, who is a member of her college diving team, was in Puerto Rico when the earthquake struck. She was in good company with about forty kids there, but she called me and was upset, telling me about the problems. I must have asked Saint Anthony a thousand times, "Please Saint Anthony, bring her home!"

The next time I heard from her, she was happy. They had gotten a generator and were able to send out for pizza. They even celebrated her birthday there. And finally the airport opened. It was closed for several days through that crisis, but their flight home was cleared for the next day.

Thank you, again, Saint Anthony!

GARY

My mother was a Catholic and my father a Protestant. My parents let me make my own decision. So I was baptized when I was ten years old. I *chose* to be a Catholic. I was very close to my mother's mother, and she wanted me to become a Catholic, and I felt it was the right thing to do, and I'm happy I did.

Years later, with three kids in college, I lost my job. A lot of people told me that since I was over fifty, I would *never* get another good job. However during this time, I relied on my faith, prayed the Rosary every day, and soon I got a *better* job.

There is a saying, "When one door closes another one opens," but this experience has taught me to be receptive to whatever is going to happen and not to rule out any possibility that may come my way. And always, I ask the Holy Spirit to guide me to holiness.

When I entered the Catholic Church in the 1940s, Carnegie had a Polish Church, an Italian Church, a German church, and an Irish church. I'm Italian with some English and German, so I chose Holy Souls. Of course, we have a different mix of churches today, and I continue to pray to all the saints, but especially Saint Margaret of Scotland, Saints Simon and Jude, and Saint Elizabeth Ann Seton.

And I feel a very close connection with Saint Anthony. It seems he never fails me, and these extraordinary things keep happening with him!

To show you how Saint Anthony has blessed me and my family just recently, in January of this year we were up at State College for a conference, and I lost my Duquesne University class ring. Of course I prayed to Saint Anthony, and I had not written him off, even though it was almost two months with no word.

But then I received a call from State College to tell me they found my class ring in my room, and they're mailing it to me. They found the ring behind the dresser. This to me is extraordinary because both my wife and I had already looked behind the dresser! So that just goes to show you, if you keep the faith, he will never let you down.

While prayer helps me to focus on what is really important in this life—and I try to pray the Chaplet of the Divine Mercy and the Rosary every day—I need to do the work expected of us to bear good fruit and to save our souls. This is why I joined the Knights of Columbus.[15]

The KofC has a lot of programs through which I can take an active role in helping others, like Faith In Action, Food for Families, Support for the McGuire Home, St. Anthony School Programs, Ultrasound Initiative, and Prayer to the Holy Mother for Persecuted Christians.

Jesus says, "...only the one who does the will of my Father will enter the kingdom of heaven."[16] So, I try to do the work that only I can do for the Lord, and at my final judgement, I pray the Lord will say to me, "Welcome, my good and faithful servant."[17]

JOANN R.

This is my favorite Saint Anthony story: For those who knew my mother, we knew that she elevated cleaning to a religious experience.She cleaned everything, all the time. My dad was alive then, and their place was like Grand Central. It's where we all congregated. And when the grandchildren were little, they were always running in through the house. So she scrubbed the kitchen floor "on hands and knees" every day.

My mother went to daily mass and communion. She was one of those faithful women who, if she had five seconds of time on her hands, she turned it into a prayer. And she rarely took off her wedding rings. I'd like to say "never," but I won't go that far. It could be true, though.

Anyway one night, in her ritual of scrubbing the floor, as she dumped the bucket of dirty water down the kitchen drain she saw that her diamond was missing out of her engagement ring. Some people use rubber gloves when they clean, but not my mother. She did it with her bare hands. But she was sorry now and feared that she'd caused her diamond to go down the drain. She was upset and started to cry as she told us kids (adults now, but still her kids) what had happened, and she asked us to pray to Saint Anthony to help her find the diamond. Some of us really thought it was gone.

Like I said, cleaning was a religious experience for my mother, and in the days after this, she seemed to be even more solemn, more deliberate in scrubbing. And all this time, her kids are praying to Saint Anthony, and she's making a novena. We moved the kitchen table, and we had the kitchen chairs in and out. And she moved it too, to clean.

Over a week later, she gets down in her scrubbing position, again wiping the floor with her rag. And she felt this scraping under the rag, and she's like, "What is *that*?"

She picked up the rag, and her diamond was in the rag! There it was!

It had been gone over a week, and, one day, there it was in her rag. The diamond was there, and she believed that Saint Anthony put it there. She always believed that he put it there for her to find because it was so meaningful to her. And she knew how hard my dad had to work to buy that engagement ring, you know?

My mother's faith in Saint Anthony has rubbed off on at least one of her grandchildren. My nephew Anthony is a newly commissioned officer in the United States Marines. I once gave him a Saint Anthony prayer card from when I visited the Basilica of Saint Anthony in Padua, Italy. He carries that in his wallet, and he can read it and pray in Italian.

When I attended his commissioning ceremony recently with his parents, our family was invited to the officers club for lunch. He was detained by some matters and arrived after we'd said grace.

He walked in and took his seat, the plate of food already in front of him, and he put his head down and prayed his grace, blessing himself before tasting the food. My mother would have been so pleased he's keeping the faith.

And he will start to be deployed, going out into this world of danger. I am invoking Saint Anthony more and more to keep him safe.

JOANNE K.

I actually had occasion to use him in the last two weeks because I misplaced my credit card, which was very worrisome. It had me in quite a panic. And I knew that it wasn't lost. I knew it was somewhere in my home, but I didn't know where I had last put it down. So after rummaging through my purse a million times, and a bunch of other places in my house, I finally sent out a call to Saint Anthony. And I went back through my purse again, and lo and behold, it was in an unused pocket of my wallet—the whole time? I swear I'd gone through every pocket in the wallet. But after I said my prayer to Saint Anthony, there it was!

There have been multiple occasions where he has come through for me and my family members—too many times to count. I just know that when I put my faith in Saint Anthony, he's gonna come through. It's just amazing—like jewelry, dear pieces of jewelry. I lost a more expensive earring that my husband had bought me for a Christmas gift. We went to dinner at a restaurant, and I had given up hope that I'd find it there, but after a prayer to Saint Anthony, I called the restaurant, and somebody had found it.

My mom was Italian—both my parents were. And Saint Anthony was *her* saint. On her kitchen window sill she kept her votive image of Saint Anthony, an embossed copper plaque that was probably from her mother. Mom would light a votive candle to him every day.

And I know that there is a rote prayer for when you lose things because my mom used it.She would make a donation to Saint Anthony School,[18] here in Pittsburgh, in his name, if he would grant her request.

So I have Mom to thank for my faith. But then, she came from a strong, strong faith background. Her mother had a grotto to the Blessed Mother in her living room!

And when my mom couldn't...like in later years, when she couldn't go to mass, she'd say her daily mass at home from her prayer book. I would hear her pray.

But my prayer is freeform. I say, like whatever the situation is, I start: "Dear Saint Anthony, please aid me in my search for this object (or whatever it is) and I graciously and humbly beseech you for your help in my occasion of need. And I truly appreciate it if you can help me find this."

Figure 3.

FR. JEROME ETENDUK

You know, Christians in Nigeria are very religious. Among them are many Catholics who believe in the powerful intercession of Saint Anthony and have received benefits from his power to recover lost items. It's something I can relate to vicariously in as much as I have not actually used the intercession of Saint Anthony as a spiritual resource. However, as a pastor in Nigeria, I interacted with members of the Guild of Saint Anthony[19] who had positive stories to tell about favors received through this great saint.

The Guild of Saint Anthony has its devotions at the parish and diocesan levels. At their devotional meetings, members have their altars set and decorated with a statue of Saint Anthony with baby Jesus. The feast of Saint Anthony is a grand ceremony for the Guild. In parishes that have him as patron saint, the feast is an all-parish affair. Some of such parishes erect huge statues of Saint Anthony at their church.

While testimonies abound of people who lost their items and recovered them through the intercession of Saint Anthony, many for whom it was an exciting experience, I personally have not actually challenged Saint Anthony. Perhaps I would take this as an occasion to have it right before me, to not only implore his help for myself and for others who are in need of my prayers, but I would preach about the powerful assistance of this great saint.

MADE MANIFEST

REV. ROBERT J. GRECCO

I have misplaced things and prayed to Saint Anthony more than once. Every situation had the same pattern—I couldn't find something. I double-checked and triple-checked in areas where I thought I'd left something and went back afterwards and found it! It is a strange phenomenon.

Yes, it has happened to me where I have looked numerous times *in the same place* for something, and I didn't see it at first. But then I would say the old prayer.

My home parish, Saint Michael the Archangel in Butler PA, had strong devotion to Saint Anthony. It was almost expected of Italians to have devotion to Saint Anthony. Saint Anthony's image was on the façade of the building. He had his own altar *in* the church, and then there was a statue of him in the vestibule. So, he was represented in three places.

Also there were the "13 Tuesdays" Devotions to Saint Anthony which was traditional with Italians. As a child I served those masses, and at each mass we kissed the relic.

I've said the prayer many, many times. You know what? I think a nun taught it to us years ago. It's just a very simple little rhyme: "Saint Anthony, come around. Something's lost and must be found."

Sometimes, though, it's just the mention of his *name*. And sometimes, not even mentioning Anthony's name, but just thinking, "Oh, I should pray to Saint Anthony."

And then I do. And when the lost is recovered, I say, "Thank you."

But it *is* a strange phenomenon.

KATHY M.

"Saint Anthony, Saint Anthony, come around. Something's lost and can't be found."

I had from my early grade school with the Mercy nuns this prayer, and any time something was lost over the years I have used the prayer.

In the past year, I've had to move. I've retired after thirty-seven-and-a-half years—moving *everything*. Imagine taking a house or taking a huge place and getting rid of *all* this stuff!

So I was at the point where I needed special documents. I needed information that had to go to Social Security and couldn't find anything. And after a couple months of this, I was still on a search for the last piece of paper that I needed for documentation, and there was a deadline!

I sat down, and I was just so bewildered as I had this whole box of different files and papers, and I said, "Saint Anthony, Saint Anthony, Please, *please* help me," and this one piece of paper slid out of a file. I picked it up.

Naturally, you know? It was the paper that I was looking for. And I just said, "Thanks Buddy."

JENNA

This story goes back to my childhood years. It may seem trivial, but I remember it clearly.

During the summer, I had swimming lessons at the local public pool. Lessons were every weekday morning so I tried to prepare the night before. I was told to put my wet bathing suit in the upstairs bathroom on the towel bar above the bathtub so it would dry overnight and be ready the next morning.

One morning, I went to put on my light blue bathing suit with the white trim around the legs and neck, but it wasn't in the usual spot. I started to get nervous because I didn't want to be late for lessons. I looked high and low in the bedroom and in the hamper. And I returned to the bathroom to look at the towel bar, behind the tub and under it. Maybe it slipped down or I missed it somehow?

The minutes were ticking by. Our house had three levels, and there were *so* many places to look! I was getting frantic!

Then I remembered to pray the prayer that my mom had taught me:

"Dear Saint Anthony, please help me find my bathing suit that is lost.
Dear Saint Anthony, please help me find my bathing suit that is lost.
Dear Saint Anthony, please help me find my bathing suit that is lost."

As I continued to search, I repeated my prayer, and I decided to check the upstairs bathroom one more time.

When I went into the bathroom I saw my swimsuit! It was on the towel bar!

I was shocked and happy to see my suit in that spot. It was a small miracle to me.

I quickly got dressed and raced off to my lesson but kept this little story to myself...until now.

DOREEN

My daughter gave me an ALEX AND ANI bracelet last year for Mother's Day—with a MOM Charm on it. I only see her a few times a year, but I made sure that I wore it when I saw her at Christmas at her house.

My birthday was a few weeks later, and we were getting together on a Sunday morning for brunch. I wanted to put on the bracelet, and I could not find it. I looked *everywhere*.

"Dear Saint Anthony, please come around. My bracelet's lost and can't be found."

I called her when we were on the hour-and-a-half-long drive down, and I asked her to look for it. She said, "You're not gonna believe what your birthday gift is!" She said she had wrapped it a few weeks before, and it was waiting for me.

When we got to her house, she said she had not found it, and she kept saying, "You're not gonna believe what your birthday gift is!"

My daughter handed me the gift, and I opened it. It was another ALEX AND ANI bracelet—with a Saint Anthony charm! She knew I *always* prayed to Saint Anthony if I lost something.

It was so ironic, and we were both speechless.

We could not find my bracelet at her house. When I got home later that day, I found that bracelet which I couldn't find for a week!

ANONYMOUS PARISHIONER

My beloved, precious mother was critically ill. It was an absolutely heartbreaking chapter. But it was also full of many, great blessings, not the least of which was being able to take care of her. Mom had always been the paragon of generosity— ever-loving, giving, and caring, ever-selfless, always thinking of others, especially her beloved children. In everything she did, Mom gave it her all, and motherhood was no exception.

She loved being a mother, and it was obvious in the countless ways she had cared for me my entire life, from infancy through childhood and beyond. I have so many memories of her sweet smile and tender touch, lovingly and patiently tending to my childhood bumps and bruises—and those beautiful, blue-green eyes, always gazing upon me with compassion and understanding, as she patiently reassured me when I was ill or hurting in my teens and thereafter. What a gift God had given me to have *her* as my mother, and what a blessing I now had to be there for Mom in her time of need.

Mom and Dad poured all their love into our family and made sure we grew up as thoughtful, faith-filled people. They insisted we be good stewards of our time, talent and treasure, and that we receive a solid education. While we were not over-indulged, they always provided for things that would be good for self-development and help us to be better people.

Eventually we each grew up and left home. I moved away and was gone a number of years before returning to my home-town and to an area close to my parents and my childhood home. The decade plus that followed was a very special time… full of family time, major life events, and mass and worship time…always enjoying and being grateful for the blessing of each other's company.

But I will never forget what happened on one particular morning during Mom's illness. I had been mostly living at my parents' house, as I was my mother's primary caregiver. Mom had many complicated and competing health challenges that were increasingly landing her in the hospital, and that one morning was no exception. I knew something bad was brewing and that we needed to get her to the ER again, and sooner than later. So, I ran around the house, gathering everything we needed to take, all the while with an eye on Mom, making sure she was as okay as possible.

Among the things I sought to gather was my cell phone. But where was it?? I reached inside one pocket, then the other. No phone. I looked in my handbag. Same result. Then I started scouring the usual places, including my car, and still no phone. My cell phone was my only direct link to Mom's general practitioner and other specialists and to our family, as well as to my corporate work, which I also needed to tend to. Then it occurred to me that I may have left it in my house earlier in the morning…

I don't even remember the short drive to my house…

At that point, my mind was racing and my heart was pounding—time was of the essence. Once home, I began to search there at an increasingly feverish pace. I kept trying to recall where I had last used my phone, first searching upstairs, then downstairs. All the while, I was thinking about my precious mother and how desperately I wanted to get back to her, and I was praying to dear Saint Anthony for his intercession, saying, "Tony, Tony, please come down. My cell phone's lost and must be found."

Yet nothing—no results. Frustrated, I headed to the driveway to make another desperate search of the car. I knelt on the driver's seat, looking on the floor, under the mats, in the pockets, and under and between the seats. I moved to the back seat, covering every inch. Now more anxious and upset than ever, I shut the car door and moved to the garage to look for my phone in there.

But something kept niggling me to return to the car...

So, I went back to my car yet again, opened the door, and there, perched blatantly on the edge of the driver's seat— in the very place I had searched just minutes before —was my cell phone!

I was totally stunned and *instantly* knew that it had been mercifully, miraculously and Divinely placed there through the faithful intercession of my beloved Saint Anthony. And I immediately began to cry and thank him and our Heavenly Father for their generosity and compassion!

MICHELLE N.

Mom was a widow in her eighties and living in a high-rise apartment. She had lost her diamond ring and some money. But we weren't as concerned about the money as her ring. She was all worried about that. That ring was very special because Dad had bought it for her on the occasion of their wedding anniversary after they had been married for some years. Years ago when they were engaged, he had given her a ring he could afford, but this present, much more eye-catching, was still just a token of his great love for her and appreciation for their indescribably beautiful life together. So she treasured this.

My sisters and even some brothers had looked for a couple weeks. We'd all take a turn.

By the way, I have six sisters and five brothers—really seven brothers. Mom had two sets of twins. One set of twins passed away about two weeks after they were born. So my Mom always used to say she had eleven children, and I'd correct her and say, "No Mom, you had thirteen," you know.

Well, my siblings didn't find anything, and so when I went over, I was determined. "I'm going to tear her apartment apart." I looked in other rooms and found nothing, so I started in her bedroom where my siblings had also looked. First I checked her dresser, So I looked on top of her dresser in all the boxes—anything that was up there, underneath her doilies, then went into the drawers one by one.

I pray to Saint Anthony every time I lose something, and I learned it from Mom. My son has also picked it up, so that if he misplaces something, he says this prayer.

Mom always used the name "Tony," for short: "Tony, Tony, look around. Something's lost and can't be found."

I kept repeating the prayer to Saint Anthony, over and over as I searched.

I went over to the bed, lifted *up* the mattress and found a couple hundred dollars!

I quickly brought that to Mom resting in the living room. She was happy!

Now, I was *really* determined and was saying the prayer over and over. I just kept repeating it. And something was telling me to go back to the dresser. I might have missed it.

Maybe it was stuck in the joints inside the drawers or maybe inside some clothes. I was prepared to dump the contents of each drawer out onto the bed. So I went over to the dresser. Amazingly, my eyes caught sight of it. There it was, *in plain view* on the dresser—right on top!Saint Anthony came through!

I'm sure I gave out a whoop, and then ran back to the living room and presented it to Mom. She was overjoyed!

And to this day, I swear. It really *was* a miracle.

Figure 4.

WITH THE INFANT JESUS

MARIA

What more could you ask for? He was amazing with the baby Jesus in his arms. I just think Saint Anthony has a beautiful place in our religion, you know. What a beautiful part of our religious history!

CHRISTINE

I have prayers on prayer cards at home that I say in the evening—prayers that my mother said and that my grandmother said—special prayers *just* to Saint Anthony.

My grandmother was Irish. She came over as a baby from Ireland, so we are Irish all the way down the line. She and my mother always prayed to Saint Anthony. Seeing them do this, the family has continued to pray to Saint Anthony. And my own children picked that up, because if they lose something, they will call me and say, "Mom, pray to Saint Anthony, real quick! I need this." And then I pray to Saint Anthony.

Each of my prayer cards has Saint Anthony's picture on the front, so I meditate. He's so, so precious holding the baby

Jesus. I mean, it's a very soft spot in my heart. When I see him holding Jesus, it just draws me to him. He's gotten me through a lot of hard times. He really has. The prayers I say to him are special prayers—there's one for just health, one for courage, and for stability too, to get through hard times. So it really helps me. He's never let me down. He's always there.

I shed some tears now, as I share with you, but these are happy tears.

ANONYMOUS PARISHIONER

I was raised Lutheran. As a young man, after I met the woman I wanted to marry and made my intentions known to her, she told me that it wouldn't be possible as she was Catholic, and I was not—and she cited some fundamental differences in our core beliefs and practices. She was delighted however, when I decided to receive instruction in the Catholic faith, a faith that I fully and enthusiastically embraced. We were married shortly thereafter.

Looking back, I realize that as a Catholic, not only did I receive my partner for life and wonderful mother of my children, but also a life-long devotion to a beloved intercessor, Saint Anthony.

My early religious training had not included instruction or focus on the saints. But my devout wife, who delighted in sharing the richness of her faith, taught me the little poem to pray to St. Anthony for lost objects or assistance, a prayer I have often invoked throughout the years and with great success. And as it turns out, my birthday, June 13th, falls on Saint Anthony's feast day as well. So, although other saints have also aided me throughout the years, Saint Anthony has always been very dear to me and remains my foremost patron saint.

So often I have pondered how Saint Anthony is depicted with baby Jesus and a handful of white lilies. What a pure and holy person he must have been that the Christ child would caress his cheek! What a tremendous model and great blessing Saint Anthony is, and how grateful I am to him for his faithful example and holy assistance throughout my lifetime!

LAURA

Honestly I can't think of a major thing I've lost, but many *little* things. And it's always been a habit for me to say the poem because, when I was a little girl, my Aunt Ruth taught me: "Tony, Tony, look around. Something's lost. Make it found."

So I always said these words when I did misplace something—which happens often.

As I said, and thankfully so, I have not had anything major be misplaced, but Saint Anthony has come through for me when I've had, you know, a piece of paper I shuffle to the wrong place or a piece of jewelry or a missing earring—things like that. Yes.

I do have one remarkable story. Recently, over the holidays, some family members were telling inspirational stories around the dinner table. My sister-in-law Giulia recounted an experience which lives on in her family. It struck me when I heard it. Everybody, in fact, was crying.

Giullia is of Italian descent. Her family is from the village of Pacentro, just east of Rome in the mostly mountainous Abruzzo region. Giulia's Uncle Tony was a child then, just two years old at the time. His parents lived in a three-story row house in the village.

One day, little Tony's mother was outside when she happened to look up and saw that her child had wandered from inside the building out onto a little ledge. Since there was no barrier, he began to fall. She immediately invoked Saint Anthony to protect her child, and he floated down into his mother's arms.

This family memory obviously made a deep impression. They share it with others because the mother very strongly called upon Saint Anthony's intercession. And the baby floated into her arms.[20]

I want to say too that I am grateful for my dad, you know. My father's middle name is Anthony, and someone along the way had given him a little statue of Saint Anthony which he keeps in his china closet.

And so you have the images of Saint Anthony holding the Infant Jesus and Saint Anthony protecting the baby, floating down. It totally fits together in my mind. Saint Anthony obviously had a love for the Christ child, and my father is such a loving father. So to me, you know, it made sense. So to me, that is a perfect fit.

RUTH

When I was a little girl, my mother taught me to pray, "Little Infant Jesus, please come down, something is lost and can't be found."

She told me, "Remember how many times you *say* that, and when you find what you're looking for, thank the Little Infant Jesus *that many times*."

ST. ANTHONY AND THE CHRIST CHILD

Figure 5.

In Urgent Need!

Karen

My mother had a deep devotion to the saints, but especially to Saint Anthony. In her later years she was suffering from dementia and was losing things frequently. We spent a lot of time praying to Saint Anthony *together* to find the various items. Sometimes they were very important things, like my dad's civil service paper or papers from the army, you know, different things that she *had* to have in order to receive social security.

Thank God, Saint Anthony pulled through, and she was able to get my dad's pension from his workplace and social security, because she was a full-time homemaker. So that was important.

Isabelle

Saint Anthony has always been a beloved saint in my family. My grandfather, an uncle, and a cousin were named Antonio or Anthony.

I invoke Saint Anthony all the time for my misplaced articles. But the prayer to Saint Anthony, *that* I remember learning in Catholic school.

Here is my story: The day before my outpatient surgery, I couldn't find my glasses. I thought they were on the dining room table where I was reading. I'm extremely nearsighted, so I had taken them off to read some material. Anyway, when I went to put them on again, they were not on the table.

I was frantic to find my glasses because I can't drive or go anywhere without them. I looked all over my condo, holding on to furniture so I wouldn't fall. It's very hard to find something when you can't see very well in the first place!

Not having any success on my own, I said the prayer I had learned years ago:

"Dear St. Anthony, please come around, something's lost and can't be found."

Within minutes, something led me to check the floor under the table, and there they were!

That's all there is to it. I've lost things before, and when I say the prayer, I usually find them shortly afterwards.

ANONYMOUS PARISHIONER

I had been shopping all day, pulled up to the front of my apartment, and just then my friend Penny pulled up behind me. She was with her sister, and I was so happy to see them. I got out right away, and we talked for a few minutes, and then I waved them good-bye.

I went back to my car to carry my purchases inside, and I said, "Oh my God, where are the keys??"

I'm searching my pockets. And my key ring is not in my purse! My purse has a compartment where I keep my keys—always—so I *always* know where my keys are. I can't imagine losing them.

In our apartment building, people are prone to losing their mail keys, and once this key is gone, it costs $100 for a new one. And *all* of my house keys and my personal keys are together on that keychain.

So I thought, "Oh my God, what am I going to do?" And I'm looking on and under the car mat and rug, I couldn't find it anywhere, and I thought, "I'll push the seat back!" But without the keys, I can't start the car to move the seat! Without the keys, I can't do anything! I could feel my blood draining, so I prayed for Saint Anthony's help.

Looking again underneath the seat with the electric wires, there's a steel frame. Everything looked black, but I could barely see a little bit of silver showing. It might be the chain. I reached underneath and there they were. I could feel them, but they were in a crumpled lump. But *how* they got tangled up down there, I'll never know (laugh)!

Once I caught sight of them, I said, "Thank you, God, and thank you, Saint Anthony, for finding my priceless keys!"

MARTHA

I appreciate that the Catholic churches in this area have many different programs. Saint Margaret of Scotland Church has a group involved in knitting prayer shawls, which I like to do, and this is where I learned of the Saint Anthony Project.

My sister Susan is a kindergarten teacher and has been for some years. A few years ago, the district started a policy of assigning each teacher a computer that was to be used only for school work, since the schools can arm the devices with security and other protection. The policy is that at the end of each school year, like in June, she has to turn in the computer.

So Susan turned in her computer when she was supposed to. And when the new school year was starting, she went to pick it up, and they told her that they didn't have it, and she felt they were accusing her of not turning it in. Susan insisted that she did, but they told her, "It's not here. We don't have it, but you can go look for yourself."

There were many electronic devices on the table and on shelves. She looked and looked through all of it, but didn't find her computer. So, she was told that she would have to pay—it was hundreds of dollars—for a new one, "because you *have* to use the special one the school gives you!"

Susan was really upset and called our mother. Then Mom called the rest of the family, all four of us, and told us what was going on and that we must "Pray to Saint Anthony for our sister."

I prayed to Almighty God and just talked to Saint Anthony in plain language telling him that this computer *has* to show up. "It's ridiculous! Susan doesn't have that kind of money. Please find it for her, Saint Anthony!"

The very next day, Susan went to school and again looked through all the electronic devices. Her computer was there where it was *not* the day before. She was so thankful to all of us for our prayers. We are grateful to Almighty God and to Saint Anthony because *somebody* found the computer.

You know, we have to keep Saint Anthony in our thoughts because he is *so* nice. He really helps us in our desperate times.

GARY

I was always fascinated by the saints, but Saint Anthony is my hero. I always go to him, and he responds. Sometimes I say a prayer from the back of his prayer card I keep in my dresser drawer. I keep another in my car, and it's either in the glove box or over the visor. But, he'll respond to your prayer even if you don't say the prayer on the card.

Sometimes at night I prayed, and when I woke up, the answer was there. I can remember losing an important paper, going to bed, and in the morning there it is! It's amazing.

A few years ago, I took my family on a vacation to Bethany Beach, Delaware. There were my wife, our two daughters and their husbands, and our four grandchildren—ages six, eight, ten and twelve. We had a couple of carloads from Pennsylvania, but all the grandchildren wanted to ride with their grandmother and me (laugh).

My oldest daughter and her husband traveled the farthest. They resided in San Francisco, and they flew in to visit his parents who lived in Delaware. Then they rented a car to join the rest of our family at the beach house, thank God!!

I went into the ocean, but only up to about my knees since I was wearing my glasses. A rogue wave came up and knocked me over. I am a swimmer, but this hit me by surprise. It knocked me on my can. I wasn't sure which end was up.My glasses were lost, and I knew I was in deep trouble. I need them to see, *period*. But I needed them to drive my family home.

My wife, children, and grandchildren were frantic. I sat down in the sand and prayed to Saint Anthony, and I told him that I had a very serious problem. "I'm out of state. I don't have my glasses, and I can't drive."

I just prayed to him, "Saint Anthony, you found lost objects that I had on previous occasions lost or that went missing, and I prayed to you, only to find them by the next day."

Lo and behold! About twenty minutes later, my son-in-law found my glasses—in the Atlantic Ocean!! To me, this was a true miracle.

I want to share my story because the thing that I was told, "Let somebody else know because it will help them, maybe restore their faith," and also, it's a way for me to return the great favor that Saint Anthony gave me!

ANONYMOUS PARISHIONER

First, I have to say this: I always invoke the Lord first, and then Saint Anthony, because Anthony's doing the finding, but he's working under the Big Man's discretion. Okay?

There are devotions I do with prayer cards (hand gesture shows thumb and index finger spread over an inch).And my residence has devotional pictures all around.

I'd rather *speak* to him, you know. Most of the prayers I say myself. Yes, I do *more* of that. I actually ask him along the way for what I need, but it's how the day's going and what problem there is at hand, or what you're asking him to find.

Here's my story when I was with the babies: I worked in a nursery, Franciscan no less.[21] I was there for five years, and I'd *still* be helping there if it weren't for the problems I had with my back. I do love *babies!*

Long story short, I had been taking care of my mother, but she had died. I had to get on the ball. I couldn't sit around leisurely. I was going to work, you know. And I was looking at all angles at what I could do. Being out of work for ten years—that's a long time.

So I saw an ad in the church bulletin that they're looking for people to help. I thought it was clerical, but it didn't specify. When I went up there, Sister was in charge. She and I talked, and she told the woman working there, "Go show her the building." So the woman gave me a tour of what I saw as a busy, caring, and well-run child care center, showing me here, there, the whole place (there were individual rooms for different age levels). When the tour was completed, Sister called me into her office and asked me, "What room do you want?"

"Room, sister?" I was surprised because I really thought I would be doing clerical work. So I told her, "I don't have any kids of my own. How about I think this over long and hard, and I'll call you back in a couple weeks' time?"

Prayer helped me discern, and then I made the call. I thought to myself, "If *this* is what God wants, I'm going for it!"

"Sister, I'll take the job."

And she was so happy to have a reliable person who loved babies. So *that's* how I ended up there with the babies. I have a lot to say about *them*. But everything was by the book. My supervisor was very firm on that, and you'd better be doing *everything* right! Then, after 3,500 hours of on-the-job training, I became a supervisor.

Anyway, here's the whole essence of this story: You know, the babies have their toys and all that. But the big thing was the *binky*! Without the binky, you know, all hell would break loose. And it did. One day a baby lost her binky. The child's mother brought the binky in the morning, but we didn't know what happened to it.

And I said, "How are we going to calm this child? There's no spare! The mother doesn't have a spare here." So we're doing everything trying to comfort the baby, to keep her calm and quiet. No way!

I examined the crib and all the bed clothes and made sure it wasn't on her in any way or wasn't on the floor anywhere, you know. And the aide who worked with me, I asked her to start looking. "We have to find that binky!"

The aide said, "I checked everything, just like you did. I went all over everything."

"I know," I agreed. It's not here, it's not *here*." And we let about a half-hour go by. In the meantime, I don't remember what we were doing, but someone was walking the baby.

Again I asked the aide, "Did you check everything?"

"Yes. I checked everything over and over, under everything, under the cribs, between the cribs—everything!

"So did I. But," I said, "You know what? I'm gonna do it *one more time*."

I went over, and there it was! Talk about losing something, and then it comes back to you!

It was on the top, well, just under the top blanket on her bed! And we had taken *all* those covers off time after time. Do you see what I'm saying? If you're *meant* to find it, there it was! And we *all* said a prayer of thanksgiving.

Saint Anthony is behind all of this. And I work on him constantly for requests and petitions. But, like I said, Jesus *first*. So God and Saint Anthony find whatever it is I'm losing.

But after the binky was found, I said, "Saint Anthony, where are you? Look at the trouble we had!"

Anyway, it's good to have friends in high places.

FAMILY *MATTERS!*

FRED

My parents were German. They were born here, but my grandparents were from Germany. I think my grandfather came over in the 1880s. I was born in 1928, and my parents gave me "Anthony" as a middle name.

When I was little and lost one of my toys, my mother, she'd just say, "Say a prayer to Saint Anthony. He'll help you find *any*thing." Then I'd say, usually, an Our Father, Hail Mary, Glory Be, and then, "Saint Anthony, pray for us."

DIANE

I would constantly instill in my children—and now my grandchildren—to call upon Saint Anthony. They have become believers, and one of our grandchildren chose "Anthony" for his Confirmation name.

ANONYMOUS PARISHIONER

My seven-year-old granddaughter participates in a before-school athletic program one day a week. The program asks the children to wear the necklace they've been given to each class.

One morning, as we got ready, my granddaughter complained that she couldn't find her necklace, and she blamed her mother for having moved it. After helping her look for it, we said the Saint Anthony prayer, "Dear Saint Anthony, come around, something's lost and can't be found."

We continued our search but without success and decided she would have to participate without it. On the way to school, we talked about seven-year-olds being responsible for things like the necklace and not blaming other people when things get misplaced. So Saint Anthony *found* for us a teaching/ learning moment.

The true *find* was the lesson that we not blame others and take responsibility for our own gear.

LAURA

I am very fond of my little dogs. Our first was Maggie, and now we have Molly. When Maggie was with us, I got her a medal for her collar, and now Molly wears the same medal. It has Saint Francis on one side and Saint Anthony on the other.

I know some might think of a dog wearing a medal as silly or superstitious, but I think that when we approach it with prayer, it's not. We pray for Saint Francis to protect our pets, and if a dog was lost, we would pray for Saint Anthony's intercession to find it. Certainly, if our Molly ran away, I would be invoking Saint Anthony's help!

What do you think of my Catholic dogs? Of course they are not baptized, and we know they don't have souls, but they are wonderful reminders of God's beautiful creation and unconditional love.

Figure 6   Figure 7

CHARLOTTE

When I first heard about this project, I thought, "Well, yes, I pray to Saint Anthony when I lose things, which is almost on a daily basis." I always say to my children and grandchildren that they should pray to Saint Anthony. And it's almost said, not quite as a lark—it's said seriously—but not particularly reverently, I would say. But I didn't realize until now how much I pray to him or count on him, like I am almost absolutely certain that nothing I pray for will be ignored.

We Italians are so attracted to Saint Anthony. I remember him even as a child. There was a picture of him that my grandmother had in her basement that hung above her mangle, this big, old-fashioned mangle (wringer) that she used to press her sheets.

Years later, I came to find out that he was Portuguese by birth, but that didn't change my loyalty to him. I think of him as a very holy, serious man connected to God in a very profound way.

Our niece is named "Antonietta" because of her mother's devotion to Saint Anthony. She is pursuing an advanced degree, loves to travel, and no matter what she does, she does very well. What a wonderful girl! I have a feeling Saint Anthony is looking out for her.

TONI

As I was being born on June 13th, Saint Anthony's feast day, my mother prayed to *him* to have an easy delivery with her first child, and she did.

I was named "Antonia" for Saint Anthony and for my mother's brother, Father Anthony Teolis, C.PP.S., ordained shortly before I was born. So Saint Anthony is my patron saint!

Each year in May, I send money to two different shrines for their Saint Anthony Novena from June 1–13. I also pray the novena by myself at that time. I truly believe Saint Anthony *does* help me with my life. I truly believe he *does* help me in my requests and for different requests for relatives and friends.

To give you an idea, I ask Saint Anthony to help me with different things throughout the day, like to keep me safe when riding my bike or driving my car.Every night too I pray this prayer to him:

"O Holy St. Anthony, gentlest of Saints, your love of God and charity for His creatures made you worthy, when on earth, to possess miraculous powers. Encouraged by this thought, I implore you to obtain for me (requests). O gentle and loving St. Anthony, whose heart was ever full of human sympathy, whisper my petition into the ears of the sweet Infant Jesus, who loved to be folded in your arms; and the gratitude of my heart will ever be yours. Amen."[22]

It is probably over twenty years that I have been praying that particular prayer daily to Saint Anthony. The prayer card became tattered, so I typed up the prayer along with my other daily prayers and laminated the sheet. The original card had the image of Saint Anthony holding baby Jesus.

Saint Anthony also helps me find lost or misplaced items. For lost articles, my mother taught us to pray: "Dear Saint Anthony please come around, something is lost and cannot be found."

The most valuable item that I ever lost was my diamond heart necklace. That was in 2008. I had put it on in the morning, and I did not know the chain had broken until later when I went to take it off. Even though I retraced all my steps I did not come up with the necklace. But I kept praying to Saint Anthony.

The next day I went back to the grocery store where I had been shopping, and lo and behold! Someone had found my necklace on the floor and turned it in to the manager. I was very thankful to Saint Anthony, and I am thankful that he is my patron saint.

TERRY CUMMINGS, O.F.S.

My mom was German and my dad's family was Irish, very staunch Irish. One of my dad's brothers became a Jesuit priest. He served in World War II as a chaplain, and his older sister became a nun, Sister Angelica Cummings, who was associated with Mercyhurst College in Erie. So our family has been close to the church for generations.

The only prayer to Saint Anthony that I knew growing up was, "Tony, Tony, look around, something's lost and must be found." I actually don't consider it a prayer. But my wife lives by it. She uses that expression ten times a week at least, anytime she can't find something.

My wife has tremendous devotion to Saint Anthony, but I, personally, would *not* call that a *prayer*. I think you can call it a plea. Yes, that's exactly what I would call it. You're asking Saint Anthony to help you find something, like, please help me find this recipe before the company gets here and I don't have the meal ready...(laugh). I know that my wife and our children count on Saint Anthony quite a bit.

Saint Anthony was a Franciscan, and I have strong Franciscan roots. I was at Saint Fidelis in Herman, PA when I was just 14 or so. It's something that I feel very connected to, and I can recite in Latin. It's part of me, and I can readily sing mass parts and phrases in Latin.

But I got the best wife, and the best kids and the best grand-kids, so I wouldn't have any of that had I gone into the priest-hood, and I was too young to decide then at fourteen, fifteen years old.

However, later in life I responded to an invitation—and a calling-—to join the Secular Franciscans.[23]It's not a secret society, so I can answer any and all questions. The forma-tion period was about two-and-a-half to three years. That might sound like a lot, but we only meet once a month at St. Augustine's in Lawrenceville.

But this has been a commitment for me for over eight years now. It's a *serious* promise to recite the Divine Office daily, although I have read from my Breviary—also referred to as The Liturgy of the Hours or Divine Office—since 1989.

There are two crosses of particular significance to Franciscans.[24]I carry the picture of the San Damiano cross— that's the one from the church Francis rebuilt. And notice that I wear the Tau cross, which is the Franciscan's scapular.

You ask me what the Tau cross means to me? I say, "*This* is my commitment!" I've gotten from people who aren't aware that I am a lay Franciscan, some think it's my first initial — you know, T for Terry!

I believe the essence of this order is poverty. Of course, Francis of Assisi adored the life of poverty, and he lived that way. He considered it was the greatest thing in the world to show your love to Christ to be able to do away with the things of the earth, you know, which is something to which I aspire, but it's easier said than done.

Figure 8   Figure 9

LYNN

Mom and Dad were both of German descent, but of different religions. They married in Pittsburgh in 1946, and since he wasn't Catholic, my mother told me that they had to say their marriage vows in the rectory.

Dad was in management with an insurance company, and every time he received a promotion, he was transferred. I remember living in Whitehall until I was in fifth grade, and then we moved to Baltimore for three years, then to Nashville. For college, I chose nearby Memphis State University, but my parents then moved on to Connecticut for Dad's job in New York City, then again to St. Louis before retiring to North Carolina. So they, and I, have traveled *some* miles.

I'm the oldest child with three younger brothers. I have fond memories of Nashville, where I lived during my high school years. There weren't many Catholics down there in 1960. Everybody was either Baptist or Church of Christ. Dad became Catholic later in life, probably, you know, once his parents died, because they were staunch Baptists. But my dad was supportive of raising us kids Catholic.

Down in Nashville my mother searched for a Catholic Church whose school had a kindergarten for her youngest child. And I joined the church choir. Mother at first wasn't sure that this church was *really* Catholic because she didn't know who Saint Henry was (laugh).

But this is when a nun taught my little brother that prayer to Saint Anthony. I thought it was so cute, him saying it, and that has always stuck with me, you know, when something gets lost: "Tony, Tony, turn around. I've lost something and it must be found."

Oh, yes! And the whole family uses it now.

In college I attended mass on campus, and my non-Catholic roommate from Memphis became interested in the faith, so she started to come along. And she became a Catholic. But that was back when, if you didn't have a chapel veil, you had to put a tissue on your head, attached with a bobby pin (laugh). I told her, "We can't go in there unless we have something on our heads. Well, here's a Kleenex!"

Mother was my support and best friend. She was devout. After Dad passed away, she became a lay Franciscan. She was a person that could anticipate what people needed. She was just an amazing woman.

CAROLE

A few years ago I left Pittsburgh and went to Maryland for the sake of my granddaughter. My son and his wife had separated, and since he had to travel with his job, he needed a trusted guardian for his teenage daughter while he was away. My visit would be for just a few months, until she turned eighteen.

I was as supportive as I could be but found that I was becoming ill. Since I have asthma, I'm sensitive to particles in the air. My own house had the proper air conditioning system, but they did not have this. I was short of breath all the time. My son urged me to seek medical advice. I learned I have eosinophilic pneumonia, a rare disorder specific to asthmatics that is not curable. The condition is monitored until the decline is enough to need oxygen and steroids. It was very frightening. I would have to leave that environment a little before my granddaughter's birthday.

But down there I discovered The Shrine of St. Anthony.[25] What a beautiful, peaceful place! It is a smaller version of Sacro Convento in Assisi, Italy,[26] and the shrine and friary are run by the Conventual Franciscan Friars.

I walked the trails through the Stations of the Cross, and the grotto to Our Lady of Lourdes with Saint Bernadette, and the area of devotion to Saint Therese of Lisieux, a rose garden. It is a holy place. Inside, in the reliquary, are pieces of the skin of Saint Anthony, which were obtained from the Basilica of Saint Anthony in Padua, Italy.

Visiting the gift shop was delightful, and I bought enrollment cards from the Companions of St. Anthony,[27] as well as small vials of blessed oil, oil that has had contact with the first-class relic of Saint Anthony, to share with my family and friends in Pittsburgh.

When I pray for Saint Anthony's help, I have little leaflets and prayers that I can say. My friends and I usually make the "13 Tuesdays" Novena up at Troy Hill, and then we're saying the novena prayers—special prayers recited together.

But usually I just *talk* to Saint Anthony, you know, like I'm talking to you, and I ask him to bless my family, bless my grandchildren. I have four grandsons. I wanted to give them a very special gift, like a keepsake. So I gave each one a small statue of Saint Anthony. These are carved from the olive trees grown in the Holy Land.[28]

Years ago, when my daughter was seven or eight years old, she went through a period when she was feeling anxious. She was sensitive to change or disruption in the activity of our busy household. So my neighbor gave her a picture of Saint Anthony that she had brought back from Italy. My daughter placed that under her pillow and started praying to Saint Anthony. She has always kept that wrinkled picture.

Now, with four sons, she and her husband maintain a very busy household, and she continues to pray for Saint Anthony's help.

She called me just this afternoon to tell me that she had been concerned about a possible health problem, but the doctor assured her with good test results. Thank you, Saint Anthony!

Figure 10.

ANONYMOUS PARISHIONER

If you think *I'm* drawn to Saint Anthony, you should have known my mother. And she is the one who got me started on him. When we moved here from our house in Green Tree, we could have joined any of several parishes nearby. But she said, "Saint Anthony's church? *We're* joining!"

It was called, "The Church of the Highways." It was not in a residential neighborhood, true to its name, but we joined the congregation of that adorable little church. And then they closed it. That was very sad. There is an eatery there now.

But we had to belong to that church as long as we were able to, you know, before they closed it, to please my mother. But that beautiful little church of Saint Anthony's was a church of hope and definitive faith for both of us, and it will always be special to me!

Jimmy M.

Saint Anthony is my Confirmation saint. I am blessed to share his name, and whenever I lose things, I immediately turn to him. He hasn't failed me once. There are countless times that I've lost little things and asked for his help.

My mother taught me when something is lost to say, "Saint Anthony, Saint Anthony, please come down. Something is lost and can't be found."

I still use that same prayer because it's childlike, and I love that. The last time I used it was at seminary. I was looking for my rosary beads and found them.

Outside of lost things, when my mother was looking to marry, every day on the way to work, she would say thirteen Our Fathers, thirteen Hail Marys, and thirteen Glory Be's along with the "Unfailing Prayer to Saint Anthony."

Consequently, my parents met. They had grown up together in the same town and had known each other, but my dad had since moved away. He came back for a funeral, and my mother was there too. She went home that day to her family smiling, and they thought that was unusual because nobody comes back smiling from a funeral home. My grandmother actually asked, "You saw *Dennis* didn't you?"

My parents struggled to become pregnant and had miscarriages. I'm the oldest child. My mother said she would pray to Saint Anthony for help in having children. And once again he interceded. So I'm very thankful (laugh)!

I didn't know any of this until after I chose Saint Anthony as my Confirmation saint. It wasn't until I was a junior in high school, when my mother shared these details about her and Dad.

Saint Anthony has watched over my family in a profound way, and I'm sure he'll continue to do so.

ANNETTE M. (JIMMY'S MOM)

When I turned sixteen, my dad gave me his Saint Anthony medal. It was the only gift I remember from my "Sweet Sixteen" party. My father's name was "Anthony," and I was told my mom wanted to name me after him and call me "Antonia," but they decided against it. Dad didn't want my friends calling and asking for "Toni" and getting "Tony." But, even so, I always considered Saint Anthony as my patron saint.

When I was about twenty-six years old, it was a point in my life when I began reflecting on my dreams and goals and wondering if I would ever get married. I worked downtown, but I felt marriage was my vocation. I wanted to marry and have a family. I don't remember how I came to possess the prayer card with the "Unfailing Prayer to Saint Anthony," but this prayer would become part of my daily ritual. I began to pray this prayer followed by thirteen Our Fathers, thirteen Hail Marys, and thirteen Glory Be's. I would pray as I walked nine blocks from my parking space to my job in the Gulf Building.

One night, about six months into this, I had a vivid dream that I was at the altar getting married to someone with brownish hair, but we were facing the altar so I couldn't see his face. A few months after that I ran into Dennis at an unlikely place perhaps—a funeral home. A classmate of ours from high school had passed away.

It had been eight years since I'd seen him. In high school, Dennis had been my date for Homecoming and Prom. He was everything I would want in a husband, but when I went to college we parted ways, so I thought, "It wasn't meant to be." My college friends can tell you how I used to open my scrapbook to his picture and sigh with lament.

It took another year, but eventually Dennis moved back to Pittsburgh, and we were engaged and married within two years. How amazing that we have such a powerful intercessor!

As an aside I thought about something else I want to share with you, and it goes back to the years I worked in town. This must have been in 1997.While taking a walk during my lunch hour, I spotted an image of Saint Anthony. I made the purchase and gave it to my dad for Father's Day. After he passed away, my mom gave this to Jimmy when he chose "Anthony" as his Confirmation name. It is another example that makes me realize how God works throughout our lives to show His Glory in powerful ways.

Figure 11.

DENNIS M.
(ANNETTE'S HUSBAND AND JIMMY'S FATHER)

"Saint Anthony, Saint Anthony, I know you are around.
Please help me as I look for this thing that can't be found."

These are the words I used to repeat as a kid looking for something that was lost. At the time, it was usually a toy or some other item that seemed to be everything to me at the time. I learned the saying from my grandmother.

Growing up near Burgettstown, PA, a small country town south of Pittsburgh, I attended Our Lady of Lourdes Catholic School and was part of a strong Catholic family. I would pray every night, usually Our Fathers and Hail Marys, to imitate my grandmother who lived with us. She would say prayers and the Rosary nightly in her room as I would get ready for bed. Every time my brother and I would be looking for something, she would say, "Pray to St. Anthony. He will find it for you."

At the time as a kid, it seemed like a great phrase to keep repeating over and over as I looked for my lost item. As I got older, the items usually became something of more importance to me such as lost money or baseballs in the field.

However, my most lasting and important prayer to Saint Anthony was given to me by my future wife, Annette. It was the "Unfailing Prayer to Saint Anthony" that is recited by many, but I had never known. I was in the process of moving back to Pittsburgh from Virginia and had a strong hope of marrying her. As I was nervous about the move and having to start a new job, she had given me a prayer card of Saint Anthony. She had given it to me to pray that I would find the job that I wanted.

I used the card daily to recite the prayer and ask Saint Anthony for intercession. However, my prayer was not for me to find a job that I wanted or be comfortable with my move back to Pittsburgh. Fortunately, I used that prayer card for over a year asking Saint Anthony to intercede for me when I worked up the courage to ask Annette to be my wife. Praying to him several times each day, I requested that he would help her to say "yes" when I asked her. Because I was very shy growing up, Annette was the *one I lost* that I had always wanted to find again. She was the love of my life, and I had been given another chance. Fortunately, Saint Anthony worked his miracle and the answer was "yes."

Until recently, I had never told that story to anyone, including my wife or family. Annette had never known that I had prayed to Saint Anthony for something that I knew would be very special in my life. I still have the prayer card today, but now I am able to recite the powerful words from memory. I still pray it daily with my family. However, the requests have now changed. It is no longer something for me that I ask.

Having matured, or should I really say, having my prayer answered, I now ask for Saint Anthony to intercede for others that I know are struggling. Oh, sure. Every now and then I still might throw a personal request into the prayer, but that is only because I have felt the power of prayers. Luckily for me, the Saint Anthony prayer started with a lost item as a child, a simple phrase that was just fun to say, and has grown into a daily prayer that I use to help others.

FOCUS!

MARY Y.

Over the years I've used several precomposed prayers, and I have also in my own words just prayed to Saint Anthony and invoked his help in finding whatever I've lost.

I learned about Saint Anthony partially from my family and from my Catholic grade school. In Brownsville I attended my wonderful childhood church, St. Peters.It is now an historical church. The school is no longer there, but I went from fourth to eighth grade there. We always said prayers and talked about the saints in school, and I learned that Saint Anthony was the patron of lost articles.

When I have lost articles in my journey of life, so to speak, maybe I can't find my wallet, or my purse might be missing. Then I would stop to say a prayer and refocus. And oftentimes what will happen when I do that is, it brings me back to clear my mind. You might go back and then remember where you have put it or where it could be, and mostly I think it helped me to stop and focus.

Here is the written prayer I say. I have transferred it to my phone so that I always have it. It's an "Unfailing Prayer to St. Anthony." Would you like me to read it?

"Blessed be God in His Angels and in His Saints.

O Holy St. Anthony, gentlest of Saints, your love for God and Charity for His creatures, made you worthy, when on earth, to possess miraculous powers. Encouraged by this thought, I implore you to obtain for me (request). O gentle and loving St. Anthony, whose heart was ever full of human sympathy, whisper my petition...(tearful)...into the ears of the Sweet Infant Jesus, who loved to be folded in your arms...

ANONYMOUS PARISHIONER

The most recent experience I had was about a year ago. I lost my wallet. My entire fiscal life was in the wallet, not to mention my driver's license and other photo ID.

And yes, I invoked Saint Anthony. I just said, "Saint Anthony, help me find it."

But I also had to use common sense because I think God gives us common sense for a reason. I just had to backtrack. I had to stop at three or four different places until I found it. And I did find it. There was one card missing, so I had to cancel it and get another one. But I wasn't out of anything.

Someone took my Discover card. There are ten cards in there, and of all the cards, they decided to take the Discover card. Why? I don't know. But at any rate, I recovered my wallet.

And another time I had the same problem with my phone. I left my phone at a restaurant, and I did an invocation. I just said, "Saint Anthony, help me find it," used my common sense, and I backtracked it. In both cases, I found what I was looking for.

ANONYMOUS PARISHIONER

I think when I misplace items, especially important ones like keys, I can become anxious and nervous because suddenly my forward progress is delayed. I get stopped in my tracks, so to speak. And being nervous, my thinking game is affected as well as how I go about trying to find the misplaced item.

Enter the Saint Anthony Prayer which I've used for years as do my children and two granddaughters. I could not even count the number of times I have asked for his help, and almost always, within a brief period of time, the item is retrieved from an odd or, at times, a very ordinary location.

Saying the prayer places me in a calmer, more grounded state of mind, reducing my anxiety and allowing me to open to the grace of Saint Anthony's guidance.

ANONYMOUS PARISHIONER

I've done it hundreds of times. I'm always losing things, but this story is the funniest one that I could think of.

Busy as I am, I'm going to the grocery store and buying some stuff for the freezer and refrigerator and bringing it home, putting it all away, and accidentally leaving my key ring in the freezer. Later on, I'm looking for those keys—for hours!

Then I got serious and said the prayer to Saint Anthony and redid my steps. You know. I just asked myself, "After I came home from the grocery store, what did I do next?"

So I checked the front door and checked everything else. And here, it was in the freezer with the ice cream!

So it might be a short story. But at least you know that the prayer worked. And I have to say that it works *every* time.

That's the only thing I know about Saint Anthony—saying a prayer to him when something is lost. My German grandmother taught me to say, "Dear Saint Anthony, I've lost something, and

I wish that you would help me find it because I can't find it on my own, and I need your help."

LYNN

Every winter I look forward to a week in Fort Lauderdale with long-time friends. Two of us are snowbirds—myself and my good friend Donna with whom I worked a number of years at a department store in Robinson. Last year, we joined three other women, all high school friends of mine.

After everyone arrived it was still too early to check into our unit, so the five of us went to a restaurant for dinner. When it came time to pay the bill, Donna riffled through her purse, then cried alarmingly, "My money is not in my purse!" She thought somebody had pickpocketed her, but I didn't think so. Honestly, there was nobody around.

From there, we checked in. There were safes for our use, but of course, Donna didn't have her envelope of money, so she was just beside herself and kept saying, "I can't believe somebody pickpocketed me!"

I sat down with her. "Let's pray to Saint Anthony." And, also, I suggested, "Let's *think* about where it might have happened." But nothing came of this because she was too distressed.

On the following morning, Donna was still upset, but something made me say with confidence, "Say a prayer to Saint Anthony, and somehow this is going to work out okay."

So then Donna was ready to focus, and we backtracked, you know, talked through where we'd been, what we had done, and importantly, where she was when she had last seen the envelope. Well, she thought about it nearly the whole day, and finally remembered, "I think I had my envelope when we were having breakfast at Bar Symon at the Pittsburgh Airport."

And I reassured her, "Okay, Saint Anthony is going to come through."

So we looked up the phone number, and she called the restaurant. Our waitress had found the money envelope on the table the previous day and had turned it in to the manager. There was no identifying information, just an envelope with plenty of cash.

Knowing the envelope was safe saved the day because then Donna was able to relax, and this allowed all of us to have a very enjoyable week in the sun.

When Donna and I returned to Pittsburgh airport, she met with the manager of the restaurant, and he gave her the envelope. He may have recognized her face because they have security cameras. The whole thing was on video.

We were amazed, though, that they had the envelope, and that the waitress turned it in and that all of the money was intact. And I said to her, "You know, that money envelope! That just *had* to be Saint Anthony's intervention. He came through!

CHARLOTTE

How many times can I say this prayer, "Saint Anthony, please help me with this?"

Sometimes I'm even embarrassed to ask him, but if it's more serious than car keys or glasses being misplaced, I say it more thoughtfully.

I wanted to visit a friend in the hospital for Christmas. She is a young woman whom I had gotten to know well through my volunteer work at a local nursing home. She is a quadriplegic. In addition to her paralysis, in October she had suffered bleeding on the brain and was taken to Montefiore Hospital, in Oakland, for brain surgery. I had visited her there. However, after talking with her mother on the phone, I understood that her daughter was transferred to a different hospital just recently, this one in the South Hills.

It was around noon on December 20th and there was *so* much traffic. Some people were driving like mad, honking their horns, and just in a hurry. And I thought, "Oh, this is so difficult to go out to this hospital, much worse than visiting her at Montefiore."

But I finally got there and asked the women at the reception desk for her room number, and one said, "We have nobody by that name."

"Oh," I said, "You *have* to, I talk to her mother almost every day. I know she's *here.*" And the other receptionist looked down at the book very carefully, and then at me. "No, we don't *have* her."

I thanked them and said that I was just going to sit in the waiting area and think and pray to Saint Anthony. They said, "Okay," and I could see that they were discussing among themselves. So I sat and prayed for ten or fifteen minutes. Then one came to me and said, "Do you think it could be that she's in a health center close by here?"

I wanted to check with my friend's mother, but I had forgotten my phone. They gave me theirs, and I talked to the mother who herself is a resident of an elder care home. She visits her daughter nearly every day, most times traveling via ACCESS, even with all the rigors involved.

As it turned out, the mother had been confused about the *name* of the place where her daughter was now. I ended up finding my friend at the health center suggested by the receptionists.

Later, I thought to myself, "It was the prayer to Saint Anthony that I can point to," because I stayed very calm through that situation. I also thought, "I am so glad I mentioned Saint

Anthony to those women too, for whatever spiritual benefit that might contain for them."

DIANE

Saint Anthony is most special to me.

As I become more aged, I rely more on him as my memory begins to fail me.

MILLY

The prayer I learned from a friend is, "Tony, Tony look around, something's lost and must be found."

I moved here from the Greensburg Diocese about fifteen years ago, and at that time I had a GPS. You know, my son bought it for me. He's so good to me. So is my daughter. When I moved in, she bought me a California closet system.

Anyway, the GPS was small enough to hold in my hand. This area was all new to me, so it was good for giving directions before this new technology on cell phones. That's how I got around!

My story is something that happened in my place. They recommend you have these air ducts cleaned every once in a while. Air ducts are set very high on the wall, and it's something I can't do myself, so I called a company and the guys came. It didn't take them long, and the job was done.

A couple days later, I went looking for my GPS and I couldn't find it. And I thought maybe one of those guys lifted it. I said the prayer to Saint Anthony to help find it. And, you know, I was going to call the company and tell them about it. But I didn't, even though I felt it was stolen.

It must have been Saint Anthony who prevented me from calling. About three months later, one of my friends came over and we were in the room where I have a chest of drawers with deep drawers. I was going to show her one of my sweaters, and I pulled out the drawer, and there was my GPS inside! I gasped. There was my camera too! This was my little camera that I *loved*, that had been missing a long time. I had forgotten about it! I remembered then that I had put them in there, but somehow I forgot about doing that, you know.

But I was being very careful. If someone was here, these precious things my son gave me couldn't be seen.

DISCOVERING SAINT ANTHONY

JUSTINE

I am a parishioner of Holy Trinity Ukrainian Catholic Church in Carnegie, on Washington Avenue. We make the perogies. Everyone *loves* them. I sometimes attend mass at Saint Elizabeth Ann Seton, and I saw the Saint Anthony Project advertised in the bulletin.

My mother had a real close friend. She was Italian, and she *loved* Saint Anthony. I was not very familiar with this saint. But I'd hear things like, you know, if you ever lose anything, make sure to call Saint Anthony.

So my first encounter was when I was helping at an event at the church with my mother. We were both helping at a funeral reception that took place in the auditorium of our Ukrainian Church.

Mom had a beautiful ring that my father purchased for her for their fortieth anniversary. And she went in to wash her hands in the ladies room. And she came out and was hysterical because she lost her ring. She couldn't figure out-—no memory—like where would this have been, and so forth.

So I immediately ran into the ladies room, and when I came out, I said that there was nothing there. One of these ladies said to me, "Did you call Saint Anthony?" I just looked at her, and she repeated, "Did you *call* Saint Anthony?"

And I said, "I don't know how to *do* that." She said, "Just call, 'Tony, Tony, come around! Something's lost, and it's gotta be found!'" And I looked at her, like, "Really?"

So, as soon as she said that, I said, "I'm going back into that ladies room." Something just made me *do* it. So I went back, and I'm calling him all the way, walking about twenty-five feet or so. And I'm calling him so earnestly.

And I went in, and there was a receptacle there. It was wrought iron, you know, fancy. So it was open, and there were paper towels in there. So I bent over and picked up a paper towel, and the first one I picked up had her ring in it. So I ran out of there. "Look! Saint Anthony!"

I had this ring in my hand, raising it like a trophy, and my mother was just in awe. She was so happy because that ring meant so much to her. Mom's Italian friend said, "See, I told you. He *works*!" And I said, "He *does*!"

And everyone there saw this. There were quite a few ladies there setting up, maybe ten or more. And I mean *every*one reacted. So this was great. I went home and told my family what had happened. My dad was thrilled. And ever since, I just feel very close to Saint Anthony.

———

I was affiliated with a hospital where I was in charge of the Education Department. When I started, there were eight instructors on staff.

One day a staff member came into my office very upset. "Oh, I've lost my keys. I've lost my keys!"

And I said, "Did you *call* Saint Anthony?"

"What?"

There was a side door where the staff could come in, and leading from there was a sidewalk and the lawn. "Where did you walk? Let's go." I just felt that we were going to find them.

So I left my desk. I was in a conference at the time, but I accompanied her, and we went out the door, and we're walking through the lawn, and I'm calling "Saint Anthony!" And she's laughing. I looked down. I saw something shiny. I put my hand down, picked up the keys and held them up to her. "Sue! Saint Anthony!"

She talks about this all the time, and now *she* shows people how to *call* Saint Anthony."

MARY J.

I talked to a friend recently in church, and I told her that I lost my gift card for Trader Joe's. So I started praying to Saint Anthony, as she suggested.

I just prayed, "Dear Saint Anthony, please find my Trader Joe's card?" I found the card yesterday, stuck away in my wallet—which I rarely do—where I had never looked for it and where I never expected to find it!

MARTIN O.

My first experience with Saint Anthony was when I lived in Atlanta, Georgia. I lost my car!

I went to pick up Miss Barbara at the airport. I had parked the car in the parking garage. I was in a hurry to get there because I was already late, and I didn't note where I was parked.

So when I finally got her and we got back to the garage, we're looking for my copper-colored Toyota Avalon, and I'm thinking, uh-oh! The garage was huge, and I had *no* idea where my car was. This was in 2011, so this was the '04 model, not my new car with that clicker, you know, where you hit the button and it answers to you?

So it's ninety-*plus* degrees out, and the humidity is up in the nineties. They call it "air you can wear." We're "sweating like stuck pigs." It's just getting unbearable because we're dragging luggage too, trying to find this stupid car.

Then Barbara said, "Stop! Just stop everything." And she called emphatically, "Saint Anthony, we *need* to find this car!"

And no sooner did she *say* that, we walked around a corner, and *there's* the *car!* And I said, "Wow, how'd you *do* that?" And she said, "That's what Saint Anthony *does*, he just *finds* things for you." And we got in the car and drove home.

But, you know, I do remember hearing about Saint Anthony when I was younger, and if you had something lost, that's the guy you would go to, but it kind of got lost in the sands of time, you know, until Barbara used it again, and so effectively. I said, "Wow I've got to keep this in mind."

Yes, that was terrible. Like I say, we had wandered around that parking garage for more than forty minutes. And it was getting really bad (laugh). We're both sweating something terrible. Atlanta heat! And it's just like I say, it was *un*bearable! Once we found the car, Barbara said, "Turn on the air conditioner. Get this thing fired up!"

ANONYMOUS PARISHIONER

I call upon Saint Anthony all the time. My mother had a huge devotion to Saint Anthony. There was a little chapel in

Bridgeville, and she would attend the Saint Anthony Tuesday night novena.

She felt that she was a kindred spirit and a friend to Saint Anthony, and so she would call him "Tony." When she lost something she would say "Tony, Tony, look around, something's lost that must be found."

She had all of her children doing this too. We all just knew that as soon as you couldn't find something, you just said the prayer. Or we would just call, "Tony!" And he knew what we were talking about, you know. And we'd find our lost articles. 99.99% of the time you found your stuff.

I married into a non-Catholic family. As a Catholic, I honor the Blessed Mother, while they do not. While I pray to saints, this is outside their realm of belief. They say, "We just go to the big guy. We go to God. We go to Jesus Christ. *Why* would you pray to saints?"

So here's my Saint Anthony story: Two of my sisters-in-law were in California in a busy shopping district and could not find a parking place anywhere. They drove around and around, but they could *not* find a single place to park.

Finally one said, "Let's pray to Saint Anthony for a parking spot, because isn't *he* the saint who's supposed to find things?" I'm sure they laughed at what they considered a big joke.

They drove around the block, and amazingly, they found an open parking spot right there. They pulled in and looked up. They were parked in front of Anthony's Dry Cleaners!

LEAD ME TO THE PLACE

JIM W.

Very definitely have I prayed to Saint Anthony, many times over! I lose things all the time, and he's been successful for me on more than one occasion. I say the short, little prayer that we were taught, "Dear Saint Anthony, please come around, something is lost and must be found."

I don't know if I can remember who taught me that, if it was in school or from a friend. Obviously *somebody* told me, when I'd said I lost something and couldn't find it, "Hey, say this prayer to Saint Anthony!" You know, it might have been my mother-in-law. And even though I may not remember who *first* told me, I've remembered to *use* this prayer. It is short and right to the point.

My children are grown now and out of the house, but a few years ago, I was planning on going to the men's retreat. It is held annually on a certain weekend in the fall, beginning on Friday evening through Sunday afternoon.

When I left home on Friday, the TV remote/channel changer was missing. I had quickly looked in all the places I thought it might be but left the house without locating it. And all weekend long at the retreat, I'm thinking, "I hope my wife and the kids find it before I return home," because there were some shows I looked forward to, and just the convenience of that remote was something I really liked. I could relax in my chair, you know.

It was a very inspiring weekend. A man I'd met there gave me a book by Saint Louis de Montfort.[29] I'd also talked with another man about EWTN.[30] At that point, I did not know what the acronym meant, but he explained it all to me, sharing with me some of his favorite programs on this television network, and so on.

It was a weekend of reflection, and I spent much time in prayer, but I admit that the missing remote was on my mind a couple of times.

When I came home on Sunday, I was in the house all by myself. My wife, according to plan, was over her sister's house baking cookies with the kids. I zeroed in on the TV set, and I didn't see the channel changer, though. So that was a clue that they hadn't found it.

That's when I used the short prayer to Saint Anthony. And something—like a voice in my head—said, "Go into your son's room and look for it."

I walked down the hall, and to the open doorway of Joey's room, looking around. I scratched my head thinking, "*Where* do I begin?" I flipped back the covers on his bed. Lo and behold! There underneath the covers was the channel changer.

It had been gone since Friday. And I now knew that my wife had to do without it the whole weekend.

Then I called my wife on the phone (giggle) and asked her, "Hon, did you find the channel changer?"

"No."

I said, "Well, I did! I've only been home twenty minutes or a half hour, and I found it!" But I said, "Thank you, Saint Anthony!"

That to me was remarkable because it was gone all weekend when I wasn't there. I can't tell *how* many times I've lost things and received Saint Anthony's help. I've lost keys and *something* said, like, "Go outside and look for them." You look down, and there they are on the walk. And you can attribute it to Saint Anthony. I know *I* do.

He's there, and he's listening to me, and I know that. I know Saint Anthony is a tremendous saint. And I love him for everything he does for me.

JUSTINE

When my dad had his heart surgery, they had a problem. It wasn't like it should have been. So now there were recurring episodes—they called it flash pulmonary edema—where he would be sitting there talking to us, and all of a sudden there were bubbles at his mouth, and he would have this sense of drowning. It's like, he was full—in his lungs! So whenever it happened—and it could happen at any time—we couldn't wait for an ambulance because he would have died at the door.

Fortunately he could walk during these episodes, at least to the point where I'd help him into the car, and then I'd race through the traffic lights. The angels had to be with me. This one place where you come up Swallow Hill Road, there are all these intersections, and I just flew through there. I always prayed, you know. "Get me there," because he would have died in the car!

So one day, I had taken Dad to the hospital like that, and he was in intensive care in the coronary care unit, and after they got him somewhat stabilized, he asked for a piece of paper and pencil. He wrote me a note.

"My wallet. lost it. $300 inside!" So my sister and I went back to my parents' home. And I want to tell you, we were *upset* because of how sick Dad was, and we knew that this was stressing him further.

I couldn't think about anything except I'm looking for this wallet. And I said, "Where could it be?" We really tore the house apart, and it was a long time, I bet an hour or more that we were looking.

Then I said, "You know what, Betty, what's *wrong* with us? Why don't we call Saint Anthony?" I had already experienced him with my mom's ring. And this was like, I don't know, maybe three years or so later.

So the layout of the house, when you go in there's the living room, then the kitchen, and a long hallway down to where the bedrooms are. Here in this hall was one of those desks that you pull the lid down, and there are little cubicles that you can pull out.

So I'm calling "Saint Anthony!" But I'm down the—you'll never believe this—I'm down the hall, and when I'm calling him, I actually felt like there was a force that was going *this* way that turned me around to go *this* way, which led me right to the desk. I opened it, pulled out these little drawers, and his wallet was in there! There was eighty dollars in it. I remember that.

"I said, "Betty, Look! Saint Anthony! Why did we wait so long?"

But we were so engrossed, you know, in getting Dad there in his illness and all, and we were afraid he might pass away. That time, though, we gave him his wallet, and it was such a relief when he came out of it.

We had to take him to the hospital several times, and then, finally, it was bad. It was *so* bad. He was *so* down. When we got into the hospital that turned out to be the last time, he took a little flashlight from his pocket. He said, "Give this to your mother. Tell her to put it on the nightstand. She's going to need it."

Then I knew he was going to die. We were getting into the elevator going upstairs, and I heard the code. And I said to my mother and sister, "That's for Dad. He's gone."

RAJKUMAR M.

So there is a place called Saint Anthony's Church in Parrys in the heart of my city, Chennai.[31] Saint Anthony is famous, and the church is famous as well.

Every Tuesday is dedicated to Saint Anthony, and you can see a lot of pilgrims coming over there—not only Catholics, not only Christians, but also Muslims, Hindus as well as worshippers from other religions will be there. And every week on Tuesday evening a special mass will be there, and that will be well-crowded and with an awesome choir. And it has always been a place of miracles. People come with a lot of problems, pray to Saint Anthony, and I have seen some of these people, and I have heard a lot of testimonies when they are healed.

So to be very specific, Saint Anthony is known to be a finder, like when you've lost something, you pray to him, and you get back that thing. But it doesn't stop there. It's more than that, because health issues get resolved. All the skin diseases have been resolved. And a lot of people who don't have a child though married for many years, praying, and they have got that.

I would like to share my story, which happened maybe five or six years ago, while I was living in India: On one evening, my family and —this includes my parents, my wife, and two small children—we were coming back from some kind of function, somewhere we went, and at the time when we returned home, it was very dark because it was around midnight or 1:00 a.m., somewhere in there. But there was also an electrical failure. It's very common there. Here in the U.S. electricity is reliable, but in India such is very common.

We were all in the car. And I lost the key to the door of my house—the main door key! I didn't know where I put it! As I said, I had my kids with me, and my parents were there, and also, it was raining. How was I going to get into my house? It was so dark, you cannot imagine the scene. I was searching, searching, everyone searching.

And at last, something sparked in me to pray. Just like that, okay? "Saint Anthony, please help me at this moment. Let me find my key."

You won't believe the immediate spark that turned me to go and check in the driver's seat below the carpet. I went there, just to move the carpet. I saw the key (laugh). It was so magical, and it was miraculous. It's a small thing, but it makes a lot of difference when I call Saint Anthony!

So on the whole, to me personally, Saint Anthony is the closest saint and always in my prayers. So it's an honor. I'm blessed to talk about Saint Anthony at this moment.

SHARON

My mom had been diagnosed with lung cancer. And it was a time when I was trying to back away from volunteering so much, because I volunteered everywhere. At one point, someone said, "You are the hardest working worker who never gets paid." I was probably overextending myself. I was raising the family, had a daycare in my home, and I would volunteer in my kids' school activities and functions, in scouting, and all that.

So this one year, I also took on being treasurer for the community softball/baseball organization. And I was collecting all the registration fees. At that time I had a minivan that had a drawer with a lock. So this one day I went to the field early, I collected a lot of fees and locked the money away, then went to watch the baseball game. And my busy life continued.

The next week somebody from the baseball organization asked me, "Did you make a deposit?"

And I'm like, "A deposit of *what*?"

"All the *money*!"

Ugh! I couldn't find it! Like *where* is this money? Naturally, instinctively, I went to Saint Anthony. "Saint Anthony, please help me find this money." I personally didn't have the extra funds to replace it if it were lost!

I shared my predicament with a couple of friends. One advised, "When you say the prayer, turn in a circle, and when you stop saying the prayer, at that point—that's the direction where you'll find what you've lost," which I had never heard before.

So I was doing everything I could, praying constantly to him to help me find this money. And I tore apart my bedroom, my dressers, every possible place that I could have put money. And I still wasn't finding it.

And I thought, I need to rip my car totally apart because I *know* I locked it in there, and I *know* I didn't take it out. Now it's getting close to two weeks of not finding it, and I'm really fretting, so I went into my car, and I took everything out of it— the mats, even the seats, because you could do that then, you know, in case it was on the rug underneath. And also I went back to that drawer, but I didn't *see* anything. But I remembered I had put the money *in* there.

The whole time I'm praying "Saint Anthony, please lead me!" Instead of going like this with my hand (feeling and patting downward), my hand went *up*! So I put my hand *up*. Well, here, because the drawer was full, the envelope with all the registration fees was tucked *up* inside. And that envelope got caught up in the springs of the seat!

I thanked Saint Anthony so much for taking my hand and turning it up. Because I wasn't thinking *up*. I'm thinking *down*. So, needless to say, Saint Anthony came through. It took a little longer than most times that I've lost and found something with his help, but when I was really desperate, Saint Anthony helped find that money.

So I made the deposit, and from then on, I said, "I'm *done*." I learned that I don't want to be responsible for money again — possibly losing it? I don't want to go through that experience again!

Saint Anthony definitely helped me find it. But, yes, that was probably the most traumatic experience of my life. And when I shared what happened, someone shrugged it off, "Oh, it's just *money*!" Yes, but it was a large amount of money that I couldn't replace at that time. So, I was very grateful.

And this was the money to pay for insurance for the kids, so if anyone was hurt and needed medical care, that would have been on *my* shoulders. So, I needed that money. Yes! It was very, very important.

I want to say too that the prayer I had been taught is "Tony, Tony, come around. Something's lost and must be found." Maybe that's irreverent though, using "Tony." But at least I called him *Saint* Anthony.

Like I said, somebody told me once that you turn in a circle while you're saying the prayer, and when you stop, that's the direction you walk. Well, that didn't help (laugh).So, don't go in circles (laugh).

Judy

Here is the little poem I've known my family and many others to use, to seek Saint Anthony's help to find something: "Tony, Tony, turn around. Something's lost and can't be found."

Of course afterward, I pray to the saint in my own words, asking for help. I find it empowering that gifts God has given to the saints down through the centuries are there for me, for us, if we have faith. I understand that the saints want to help us and want us to tell them what we need.

One summer evening, after work, I drove my best friend to a wallpaper store in Cranberry, about forty-five minutes from my home. This store has a huge inventory which occupied us for a couple of hours.

I didn't find anything close to what I had pictured, but then again there was no timeline for my dining room to be done. The wallpaper I'd put up years before actually still looked good, but I just wanted to give the room a fresh look. After leaving the store, we went to an ice cream parlor a few doors down. So it was an enjoyable, delicious girls' night out.

A couple days later, my husband and I realized that our spare set of car keys was missing. Our home is organized, so I knew I should find them in no time at all. But since they were not in the spot where we always store them, we began hunting in the sofa covers, in drawers, and every place else where keys might hide in your house.

I said the little poem to Saint Anthony, and then I prayed in my own words to him, so I *knew* that the keys would show up.

When they didn't show up soon, my husband and I learned that we can live with just one set of keys. We didn't want the expense of getting a set made because we figured that as soon as we did that, the keys would show up. Saint Anthony has that covered too!

Well, so much happened that year that needed to be prioritized, and the room redo sank to the bottom of the list. But come summer, I again turned my sights to the dining room.

So one summer evening, after work, I decided to drive to that wallpaper store. I felt compelled to go there. My husband could not understand why I would drive forty-five minutes to look at wallpaper so late in the day. He reminded me that I would spend more time driving back and forth than I would have to shop. But part of the joy for me is driving, and I *love* to look at wallpaper books. Though I'd be alone on this trip, something was pulling me there.

The saleslady greeted me at the door and asked if I needed help. I told her I wanted to look at wallpaper books, even though I did not allow much time for this. She told me to enjoy myself, and that I could stay until they put the key in the door. "I'll be cleaning up and vacuuming here, but go ahead on back." There was a clerk in the back, arranging the books on shelves, and it seemed I was the only visitor.

So I spread out the books on the large table, feasting my eyes on the many pictures and patterns. Time was flying, and now I had several books open. While standing over them to compare, I heard a voice coming from the front of the store. It was the saleslady trying to get the attention of the clerk. "Do you think I could finally throw these keys away that have probably been here about a year?"

"I think it's time," the clerk hollered back as she stepped closer to eye up my wallpaper choices. And in her next breath, she looked at me, "*What* are the *chances* that someone would come here to find keys that have been missing *that* long?"

I was stunned, but somehow the words came out. "Do those keys have a McElwain Motors key tag on them?"

"They sure do!"

All three of us could hardly believe what had happened then and there. While some may look at this as coincidence, I knew that Saint Anthony was responsible. He made me wait this time, but he still answered my prayer.

ANONYMOUS PARISHIONER

It happened *just* the other day. And what's *funny* is, whenever anyone loses something, everyone says, "Please Saint Anthony, help us find it."

Well, the other day, I was looking for a *major* credit card in my purse. And I forgot that I had taken a brand new purse that I've had, and for some unknown reason, I put my credit cards inside *it*.

I looked in the house and I looked in the car, and I said to myself, "Just *cancel* all these cards," and I thought about that...and I said, "Saint Anthony!" And I started laughing. I said, "*Please*, this would be very, very *hard* for me to cancel all these cards." I had about six *major* ones, plus! What could be done about this? You know, what could be done about this??

Believe it or not, at *that* moment I looked at that other purse. Then I thought, "I used that yesterday for the first time. Look in there." And, of course, the cards were inside!

So *yes*, he *does* these things. You know, I think people just fall back on it. They *know* he *does* these *things*.

And I thanked him. You *have* to thank him. Say, *Thank* you! "You do things like *that*?? We should *all* pray to you."

L.H.

I absolutely pray to Saint Anthony and have through the years. The experience I remember most was our first Christmas—and it wasn't even a whole year that my husband and I were together.

That first Christmas he bought me a beautiful diamond pendant. I had it for a couple of months, and all of a sudden, I could *not* find it. And I was devastated because I knew it was expensive, and so I prayed to Saint Anthony, you know, every morning. I didn't think I had *lost* it. I kind of knew it was there in the house, but I wasn't sure *where!*

I have a little prayer card with his prayer on it. It sits on my jewelry box, as a matter of fact. It might have been the JMJ Catholic Book Store in Bethel Park where I picked up this prayer card. It's laminated, you know. I like the depiction where they show Saint Anthony usually holding the child Jesus and a lily.

And, every morning I prayed, and wouldn't you know? That thing turned up in just a few days! It was somewhere, where I had put it. I just *forgot* that I had chosen *that* particular place. And I was so thankful then that it turned up, I prayed again to Saint Anthony, "Thank you, thank you!" You know.

My reasoning was that because it was a diamond, I hid it somewhere that if a robber would have come into the house and looked in the place where you usually keep jewelry, it would not have been seen. And since it was on a gold chain, I didn't want the chain to get twisted. So, I had a cupboard where I kept supplements that I would take occasionally but not on a regular basis. I had pressed a big thumbtack into the inside of the door, and that's where I hid it. Yes, I did a good job of hiding it. And that's where I was led to look.

I know Saint Anthony works because he *found* that thing for me. God only knows if I would *ever* have come across it? It might have been years!

ANONYMOUS PARISHIONER

I wear a gold chain and gold Blessed Mother medal from Italy all the time, and one day I noticed it was missing. Now this was a good many years ago.

I had no idea where it was. It could have been in the house, so I started searching and searching as you do, looking here and there, under things, jewelry boxes, over and over again. So I decided to pray to Saint Anthony: "Saint Anthony, please help me, if it's your will, to find this medal that is precious to me."

I was baking and opened the oven door, and there was the medal and the chain! It probably had dropped off of my neck the last time I'd used the oven. But it was in the space created at the back when you open the oven door.

I really attribute finding it to Saint Anthony. You know, I almost gave up looking for it, but that day, when I saw it, I said, "Thank you, Saint Anthony, for guiding me to find it," because it would have been hard to see. But for some reason, that day, it popped out at me. And I still pray to him in thanksgiving for things that he has helped me find, little things here and there.

But, yes, it doesn't hurt to try. As Scripture says, "Keep asking, keep praying. Don't lose heart."[32] You know, *pester* him! In other words, like in the gospel this past week about the judge and the widow who kept pestering, pestering, pestering him for something that she needed. Finally the judge gave in and answered her request. That's what Our Lord wants us to do—keep pestering Him. So keep pestering Saint Anthony if you lose something!

A Season Under the Heavens

PAUL

My wife doesn't use her cell phone that often, but it comes in handy for emergencies. And if we want to communicate, like if we're in South Hills Village or someplace where we need to get in touch with each other, it's nice to have them there.

This fall, all of a sudden, she couldn't find her cell phone. She thought that I put the phone up for recharging, and I couldn't remember putting it up for recharging. We looked all over in my computer room, where we usually recharge our cell phones. We looked in the living room, on the table, in a cabinet we have, through all the coats in our closets…all through the house really.It wasn't in any of those places.

This was going on for *three* weeks! We couldn't find it! We didn't know *where* it could be! So I said two Hail Marys and the Our Father and asked for Saint Anthony's help. That night we went to the truck festival—that food truck rally—at SSJ (Saints Simon and Jude Church), and it was *cold!*

My wife was cold, and I usually have extra coats in my car for emergencies, in case we need an extra coat. Her coat was in the trunk, so I got it out for her.

When she put it on and put her hand into the coat pocket, out popped her cell phone! *All* this time her coat was in my car with the cell phone in the pocket, and neither one of us thought to check the car. And it was surprising to find the phone *then*, because we were *so* cold, we'd forgotten about the lost phone until it dropped out of her coat pocket.

I learned to pray to this saint through my mom. She's Italian. My wife's not Catholic, she's Presbyterian. So she didn't say, or I don't think she said, any prayers to Saint Anthony. But I did.

HELEN

My husband Ramesh and I are here on a six-months visit from our home in Satara, India, located in the Sahyadri Mountains. It is famous for enchanting blooms of seasonal flowers that grow on the Kaas Plateau, UNESCO World Natural Heritage Site. But we came to Pittsburgh for an extended visit with our son throughout summer and fall 2019.He now lives and works in Pittsburgh, and he has been a member of Saints Simon and Jude Church at least a couple of years. He rents in a nearby apartment building. My son selected this place for our convenience, so that the church should be walking distance for us.

Since July we started attending SSJ church regularly and met so many wonderful, loving brothers and sisters in church during mass and fellowships. We never ever felt that we are away from our country.

On Wednesday 20th November during the fellowship breakfast, I saw a poster advertising the Saint Anthony Project. "Have you lost something and prayed to Saint Anthony to find it?" I was so happy to read this because it was not once, but *several* times I have prayed to Saint Anthony to help me to find what I had lost. My prayers were always heard, and I found what I had lost.

I am an ardent devotee of Saint Anthony and have been from my childhood. I was born and brought up in the Catholic culture and environment under my parents' tender love but strict vigilance. We strictly followed the rules and prayers and Bible studies. My mother had a special prayer to Saint Anthony if she lost something. She taught it to me, and it was made mandatory for me to offer prayers after I found what I had lost.

Let me share my recent incident: Before our trip to the U.S., some months ago it was my son's birthday. So I had made for him some of his favorite recipes of sweets to send him by parcel. The parcel was sent from India to Pittsburgh, USA through our courier agency. I had not informed my son about it as it was a surprise for him.

The day he was to receive the parcel, he was traveling. He did receive indication of the parcel being delivered, but when he returned, the parcel was nowhere to be found. He inquired of the courier company who told him that the parcel was delivered at the door. When I inquired from my courier agent in India, I was sent a photo of the spot delivery. In other words, the package was delivered, but he didn't receive it.

I was very sad and immediately started praying to Saint Anthony day and night, asking him to help my son to find the parcel. Days and weeks passed, and my son had lost all hope of getting the parcel. But I had all hopes that Saint Anthony would surely help me, and I continued praying to Him. I did not lose faith in him and kept praying in anticipation that one day my prayers will be heard. Here is my prayer, which I learned from my dear mother:

Saint Anthony, perfect imitator of Jesus who received from God the special power of restoring lost things, grant that I may find (name the lost thing) which has been lost. At least restore to me peace and tranquility of mind, the loss of which has afflicted me even more than my material loss. With this favour I ask another of you, that I may always remain in possession of the true good that is God. Let me rather lose all things than lose God, my supreme good. Let me never suffer the loss of my greatest treasure, eternal life with God. Amen.

Over a month passed. One day my son happened to meet the neighbor who was a friend, staying in the next apartment. He told my son that there had been a parcel at his door for many days, and he pulled it into his apartment for safekeeping, but after so much time, he had forgotten about it. Seeing my son, he remembered.

My son was very surprised. He was expecting a small parcel, but this was large and weighing nearly twenty pounds! My son was overjoyed. He opened it, saw everything was intact, and snapped a photo and sent it to me.

How happy I was! I believe that the guardian angels protected my son's package and that Saint Anthony used my son's neighbor as a mediator to find his package. It was a great miracle by Saint Anthony!

And I'd like to invoke Saint Bonaventure,[33] He said to ask the Wonder Worker with confidence, and he will obtain what you seek.

"Saint Anthony, pray for us all!"

PATTY

I pray to Saint Anthony on a regular basis because I tend to misplace things. I'm always distracted, so I'm always misplacing something. Generally I get an immediate answer. But there have been two occasions I'd like to tell you about, when I've lost something extremely important to me that I *didn't* get an *immediate* answer, but I received answers after a long time. There was a scapular that I wore all the time. I bought it in Lourdes on a pilgrimage. And later, when I had serious health problems-—I was diagnosed with breast cancer-—the scapular would become even more important to me.

I had to have many tests, and at every appointment, whether it was for a biopsy, MRI, or even consultations with oncologists and surgeons, I was made to wear the standard hospital gown and, of course, I was not allowed to have *anything* around my neck. So I kept my scapular clasped tightly in my hand.

My first surgery was a double mastectomy, which was very difficult. Following this, I had four additional surgeries in twenty-three months including a mass removed from my liver. It all would have been unbearable were it not for my faith. At every appointment, and I had over a hundred doctor appointments or tests during this period, the scapular was the hope I grasped onto.

Recuperating from all this was a long period, resting in my home, and with medications and treatments, and still visiting doctors. Somehow, I lost my scapular. I didn't think I left it in a doctor's office but wasn't certain, so I started praying to Saint Anthony.

The standard prayer that I was taught when I was a kid is what I use: "Great Saint Anthony, come around, I lost my scapular, and it can't be found." I don't have anything more sophisticated than that.

I went to Catholic school for eight years, my first four years at Holy Trinity, a Slovak church and school, then grades four to eight at Saint James, run by the Sisters of Charity from Seton Hill. I said the prayer probably several times.

Well, he didn't come through. The guy did not come through (laugh). I was looking for it for, oh, probably over a year. And at that point, you just don't look for it anymore. But he's been *so* good to me, so (laugh), I didn't hold a grudge.

Two years after I lost my scapular, I decided to clean out some of my drawers of anything that didn't fit or that I didn't want anymore. My plan was to donate what I no longer needed to St. Vincent de Paul.[34] So I was opening drawers. It was like a shopping spree because there were tops I hadn't seen in a while and forgot I had. And I tried on a top that I hadn't had on for a long time. I always liked this top, but it was maybe a little tight, and I thought, "Well, I'm going to try this on, and if it doesn't fit now, it's going." It *didn't* fit.

And as I took it off, the scapular fell out of it from the last time I tried it on! And I could not believe it. I absolutely could *not* believe it. So, he made me *wait* for it, but Saint Anthony paid off.

Now had I *not* tried that top on that day, I would have given that top away with my precious scapular inside. So, I do attribute this to Saint Anthony, who is known to guide us to our lost objects.

I remembered the prayer of thanksgiving the nuns taught me, after an object is found, "Great Saint Anthony, you came around, found my scapular, and I thank you, since you made me find it."

I had a rosary that was my mother's. It was given to her by a friend, and it was distinctive with its blue-tinted beads. Of little value monetarily, my mother cherished this rosary greatly, no doubt because it was from a place she longed to visit. Ironically, it was from Lourdes, France, as was my scapular you've just read about.

My mother passed away in 2004, and I treasured her rosary because she handled the beads. So I put it into my purse, and that's the rosary I would use if I needed it at church, or in the car, or wherever.

Well, at some point, I realized I didn't have the rosary in my purse. It was a terrible feeling when I went to reach for it and I didn't have it, and I had *no* idea where I'd lost my mother's rosary beads. So, I prayed to Saint Anthony: "Great Saint Anthony, come around, I lost my mom's rosary, and it can't be found."

Thinking I'd probably left the rosary at church, I made a call to the administration office. I was told by a sympathetic voice that it was not in the Lost and Found. I drove up to the church and went through the Lost and Found in the closet and in the box in the hallway where people often placed things they found. The rosary wasn't there. I was disappointed because Saint Anthony had not come through and sad because I'd lost touch of my mother's rosary. It was like a piece of her.

A couple of *years* later—it was in 2017-—I was invited to do a presentation at Saints Simon and Jude Church in the social hall for Christian Mothers. My talk was on Fatima. I was there, in Fatima, on October 13, 2017-—the day of the 100th anniversary of Our Lady's final apparition and the Miracle of the Sun.

So I went up early to set up. I wanted to make my presentation come to life. I wanted to share all of the beautiful photographs I'd taken of Fatima and share my experiences, but the podium had no microphone.

I called Deacon Jim and asked, "Do you know where the microphone may be?" He said, "Look over in the church administration building." The Director of Music, Tom Octave, was on hand for an evening service, and he walked over with me to unlock the door. Deacon had told me the drawer to go into, "in a chest, on the left as you walk in the front door."

I opened that drawer. I didn't see a microphone. There was little stuff piled in there, and I moved some of it aside to see if the microphone might be at the bottom, and there was my mother's rosary! I gasped. I just absolutely couldn't believe it. It is so distinctive—definitely mine.

You know, there would *never* be a reason for me to open that drawer in my life, so I believe that Saint Anthony and the Blessed Mother together helped me that day. It was amazing! "Great Saint Anthony, you came around, found my mom's rosary, and I thank you, since you made me find it." I also give credit to the Blessed Mother, because, you know, the rosary was from Lourdes. And I was giving a presentation on a Marian shrine.

I'm so fortunate to have gotten those rosaries back because, after a certain amount of time, the church always donates anything that is left behind. You know, glasses go to one place, gloves to another, and rosaries to another.

Our business manager Chris explained further, "Patty, when we were donating all of these items, rosaries and other things, I noticed there were a couple pairs of rosaries that I thought, "You know, these look like somebody's really going to miss them. I'm going to hang on to them."

And she put them inside that drawer.

Figure 12.

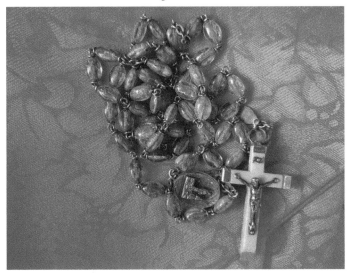

Figure 13.

Do Diligence!

Deacon Jim

Often I lose something and pray to Saint Anthony, and sure enough, it turns up. But I have one experience that stands out.

It must have been three or four years ago. My son was getting ready to go into the final phase of his Master's program at State College, and he would need to stay up there for about a week with his group. It so happened that a few days beforehand, we had a pretty decent snowfall.

So he went out to shovel the snow. Later that day, he noticed his wedding ring missing. He and his wife searched the entire apartment but didn't find the ring. And despite that he wanted to conduct a more thorough search, he had to leave.

I was in the hospital at the time, but after my discharge, I heard about the lost wedding band and that our daughter-in-law was pretty distraught over it. So my wife and I decided that we would go look for it. We knew that our son had been shoveling and thought that it could be buried in the snow.

I wanted to come up with an unfailing plan. I have a pickup truck. So I brought the pickup truck over, and I thought that we would shovel all the snow on his front lawn into the cargo bed, then park the truck in the garage until the snow melted. That would surely turn up the ring.

So there we were, my wife and I, doing what any good parents would do, I guess—out in our son's front lawn shoveling his snow into the back of a truck. We started at the place where the snow was mounded, figuring that's where he had shoveled. Still having a long way to go, I remember stopping and praying, "Saint Anthony, I need help." Yes. A lot of times I cut to the chase. I just say, "Saint Anthony, I need help." And shortly after saying that prayer, my eyes caught sight of a small circle melted into the snow!

I think one of the things to consider as to why a lot of those prayers are answered is that when I pray in this way, I relinquish control. And when I relinquish control, one of the things that happens is I tend to think more clearly. By putting it into God's hands or Saint Anthony's hands to intercede, I think we approach it more calmly. By praying to the saints and praying to God, then we attain peace. And by attaining that peace, we are able to do more.

And so I went down below that circle, and the ring was on the grass underneath the snow. What had happened is, probably when his hands got cold, his fingers contracted. As he was shoveling, the ring flew off his finger. And when it landed in the snow, the ring was still warm, and it melted down into the snow and left an impression.

Yes, my wife and I were prepared to shovel the whole front lawn. But, thankfully, our work was cut short. I told my wife and my very happy daughter-in-law that the finding of the ring was due to those prayers.

MARY C.

My story took place on August 20,1998. I'll never forget this miracle! I went shopping in the afternoon. It was a large shopping trip buying many groceries including a roast beef that I planned on preparing for that night's dinner. My husband and I are parents of four children.

I remember walking through the SHOP 'n SAVE, and I was picky about what I served my family, so I took my time selecting various produce for a salad, and I examined many pieces of meat on all sides until I found the one that was most pleasing.

Up and down all the aisles, I drove that shopping cart until it was nearly full. Then I unloaded all my selections at checkout. I headed home, unloaded all the groceries, and then started my dinner by peeling potatoes, washing all the veggies for a salad and preparing the meat. When my husband came home, we all enjoyed a wonderful dinner.

At some point while cleaning up the dishes, my hand, more specifically, my ring finger, was stuck on the tea towel. Looking down, I realized the towel was attached to the prong of my ring— my diamond engagement ring. Taking a closer look, as I tried to release the towel from the prong, I was shocked to see my diamond was gone! I was devastated and in a panic as I tried to figure out how to go about trying to find my missing diamond.

I remember calling my mom to relay my sad news and ask for prayers. My husband and I decided to retrace the steps of my day. We started to backtrack the last hours, going through the sink, next was the garbage—potato peels, celery peels, mushroom peels, meat wrap, etc.

We looked in the refrigerator, grocery bags, and we opened and searched every cabinet where I had placed food. We walked throughout the house, the bathroom, the basement, and the path from the house to the car. Then we searched the car. We searched thoroughly. And though we couldn't be certain it wasn't at home, we decided to drive to the grocery store.

It was an absolutely impossible task! We spoke to several employees, trying to find out if anyone possibly found and turned in a diamond. I retraced every section, every shelf I remembered stopping for groceries. One of the most frustrating areas was the produce section because all of this sat on a green AstroTurf-like sheet on top of grates—with holes! If the diamond was lost there, then it *is* lost. It would certainly have dropped through.

After checking at the meat department and all up and down the aisles, our last stop—and our last hope—was the checkout lane. There were customers in line, so we tried to move around them. We quickly explained our quest to the cashier. I bent down on my hands and knees under the Pin-Pad. Behind where the cashier was standing, I saw some accumulated dust/dirt. I saw something glittering and reached my hand to it. To my shock and surprise, it was my diamond! You cannot imagine how elated I was! My prayers were answered and I was extremely thankful.

On my way home, we stopped at my parents' home. I relayed the news to Mom and Dad. My dad said very casually, "I *knew* you'd find it. I've been praying to Saint Anthony and Saint Christopher."

Other family members had also assisted us in saying prayers. Given the circumstances, I truly, truly feel this was a miracle and an answer to all our prayers.

DEALING WITH LOSS

REV. ROBERT J. GRECCO

When we preach about Saint Anthony on his feast day, I, as well as other priests, remind people that it's *one* thing to pray to have returned *objects*. We need to put into Saint Anthony's hands those who have left the church and pray for them, asking for his intercession in bringing back the lost *souls*.

ANONYMOUS PARISHIONER

Well, I did pray to Saint Anthony one time I lost my keys. I was at home at the time, and I just said, "Saint Anthony, please help me find my keys." That's all I said, and I found them within maybe five minutes, like right then and there. And I said, "Oh my goodness, Saint Anthony helped me out." I was really surprised. I was thinking, "He answered my prayer so quickly," you know? And that was good.

I was in church one day, and Father Grecco was talking about his home parish. And he's the one who got me started to talk about my loss. He said, "If you lose something, *any*thing," he says, "Please pray for that to Saint Anthony."

And so after that, I thought, well, maybe if I pray to Saint Anthony, maybe he's going to help my children to realize that they were brought up Catholic.

My grandson was going to mass. But he went to college, and now he does not go to mass on Sunday anymore.

Kathy M.

When you live to be as old as I am, God puts in your path many broken, wounded people.

When I was watching EWTN recently, there was a program in which the priest posed this question: "If *you* could be a patron saint, what would you want to be the patron of?"

I answered right away—the walking wounded!

"Saint Anthony, Saint Anthony, come around. Something's lost and can't be found." Indeed! And I was one of the lost—out of the church for a long time.

So, "Saint Anthony, Saint Anthony, come around. I was lost, but now I'm *found!*"

So now I pray for people who are out of the church. And this can happen even in our own families, that children are raised Catholic, but they don't practice the faith. And these are the people I pray for.

I know that, even among people who are not in the church though, I have heard from their mouths, "Saint Anthony, Saint Anthony…"

And if this can be the way that they will find…?

If Saint Anthony can be the instrument the Lord uses to bring them back, I'm going to hang on to that and accept it. So I started to intercede to Saint Anthony in special ways. This Saint Anthony Project brought me back to something that I have not done for a long time—a more firm and structured praying to Saint Anthony. So I now have prayer cards and the chaplet.

Here! This is for you! I am giving you this one-decade rosary with Saint Anthony's medal. It's from the Franciscan Friars of the Atonement.

I am now a St. Anthony Mission Partner with the Seraphic Mass Association, supporting the work of the Capuchin missionaries.[35] They have a local office, and I love that they seek my prayer requests and that the community joins in prayer for my intentions.

Figure 14.

ANONYMOUS PARISHIONER

I am writing to tell my experiences with Saint Anthony.

I have asked Saint Anthony for help when I lose items for years. Ninety-nine percent of the time, I find the item. There was one occasion when I didn't recover the item, but I had a clear message of what I had done with it and that it would not be recoverable. So that gave me peace also.

Because Saint Anthony was always so extremely reliable in helping me find what was lost, I started to feel that lost items should not be my focus. Still I do ask him to help me find lost items, but I moved on to praying for my loved ones.

These are just my own words, but I've found these prayers to be very powerful:

"Through the intercession of Saint Anthony, I pray that my children will always find their way to their Heavenly Father."

"Through the intercession of Saint Anthony, I pray that my children will find God's purpose for their lives."

"Through the intercession of Saint Anthony, I pray that family members and friends whom I've lost-—who have died— will find their way to heaven."

KAREN

I have lost many things in my whole life, but the thing most recently that I'm afraid of losing—that I've prayed to Saint Anthony for—is my hope and faith in people.

Having our people respond to my request to get involved with Bible study, with home Bible study/living room church, is something I've been challenged to do. To start up and to kindle that fire in our people is a great challenge, and I'm being very humbled by this experience.

I had planned a Bible study group, and I came on like gangbusters! Putting a Bible study together has been an inspiring experience for me, and I hope for others to become involved since being involved in Bible study helps us enrich our lives. And I'm thinking that there are so many people in our church who have been prayers and leaders, people that I've seen who have been very devout through the years. I had hopes that from these people, we may be able to start up, you know, a living room church. In fact, we've had several meetings with small groups of people.

So I've been very hopeful until this last meeting that I had planned. I was going to show potential leaders how to *start* a Bible study group. I had planned with the best materials—I'd created a manual for leaders that I was wanting to pass out and go over. The manual is 80 plus pages of inspirational prayers, ideas, and so forth.

I'd called and invited people to come to the meeting, and various people said they were going to come. And so I had the room open here for the meeting. No one showed up!

So I did go back over to my office, and at that point I was very disheartened. I was actually crying that *nobody* came. This was in October.

So anyway, as I'm in the midst of my crying or whatnot, I remembered that I'd tucked inside my desk drawer my prayer to Saint Anthony. It is a litany that I use at times, when I lose things, but this was more, not losing a *material* thing, but losing a hope and a faith.

And so, I got this out. And I said my prayer to Saint Anthony, and when I was done, I put the prayer book that I had to Saint Anthony back into my drawer. As I closed the drawer, I looked over to my phone. My phone has a red light, and it's blinking! And I listened to the message, and the message is somebody that feels that he could be a leader and wants to talk to me, although he could not make the meeting on that particular day. So, you know, it was just an answer to prayer, and I called this gentleman back and set up a meeting with him.

I then went to my computer to continue my work, and on the computer is another person that wants to do something, but could not make the meeting and wanted to connect with me, and so forth. So, what can I say, but, you know, the lost had been found.

These messages restored my hope, and my faith, and I really feel that, you know, Saint Anthony's intervention is going to help me because I'm realizing that this is bigger than me. This is not *about* me! It's not about a job. It's about Jesus and about learning more about Jesus, and it's about a faith and a hope and a love of Jesus that can't be stopped. So this *will* go forward, and I learned Saint Anthony is going to help me.

MARIA

Oh, he's *so* tired of hearing from me. Are you kidding? He's going, "You, *again*?"

You gotta go to Sant' Antonio! He's a good person. But I always say, "Saint Anthony! Where are you today? Are you hearing me?" Because sometimes I've been *really* desperate, you know, looking for house keys or car keys or whatever. But he comes through. You always find them in the *last* place you look (laugh).

I just pray in my own words, "Saint Anthony, please help me find this," or, you know, "Are you keeping this from me to make *sure* I won't do it again?" And after I find something, I just say, "Thank you," and again, "Thank you."

I don't recall losing anything of material value. There's nothing really that I can think of. There are times though when I'll say to Saint Anthony, "I'm losing..." I shouldn't say my *religion*. I'm *not* losing my religion, but, "I'm *losing*, maybe, faith in some*one*."

So, "help me to *find* that again. Help me to find that in *me*."

So, I keep praying because I lose everything all the *time*, but not just physical things. Sometimes, you know, what's in your *heart*, you're losing control of *tha*t, and you want it back.

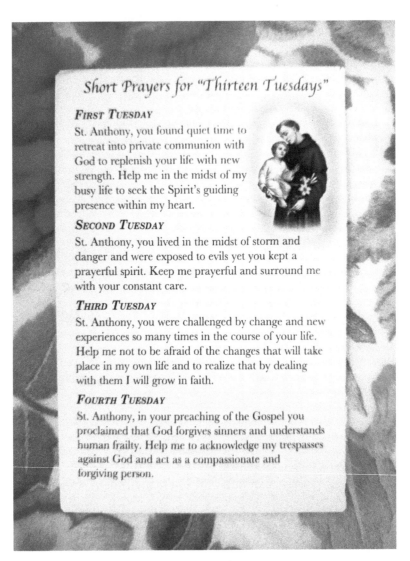

Short Prayers for "Thirteen Tuesdays"

FIRST TUESDAY

St. Anthony, you found quiet time to retreat into private communion with God to replenish your life with new strength. Help me in the midst of my busy life to seek the Spirit's guiding presence within my heart.

SECOND TUESDAY

St. Anthony, you lived in the midst of storm and danger and were exposed to evils yet you kept a prayerful spirit. Keep me prayerful and surround me with your constant care.

THIRD TUESDAY

St. Anthony, you were challenged by change and new experiences so many times in the course of your life. Help me not to be afraid of the changes that will take place in my own life and to realize that by dealing with them I will grow in faith.

FOURTH TUESDAY

St. Anthony, in your preaching of the Gospel you proclaimed that God forgives sinners and understands human frailty. Help me to acknowledge my trespasses against God and act as a compassionate and forgiving person.

Figure 15.

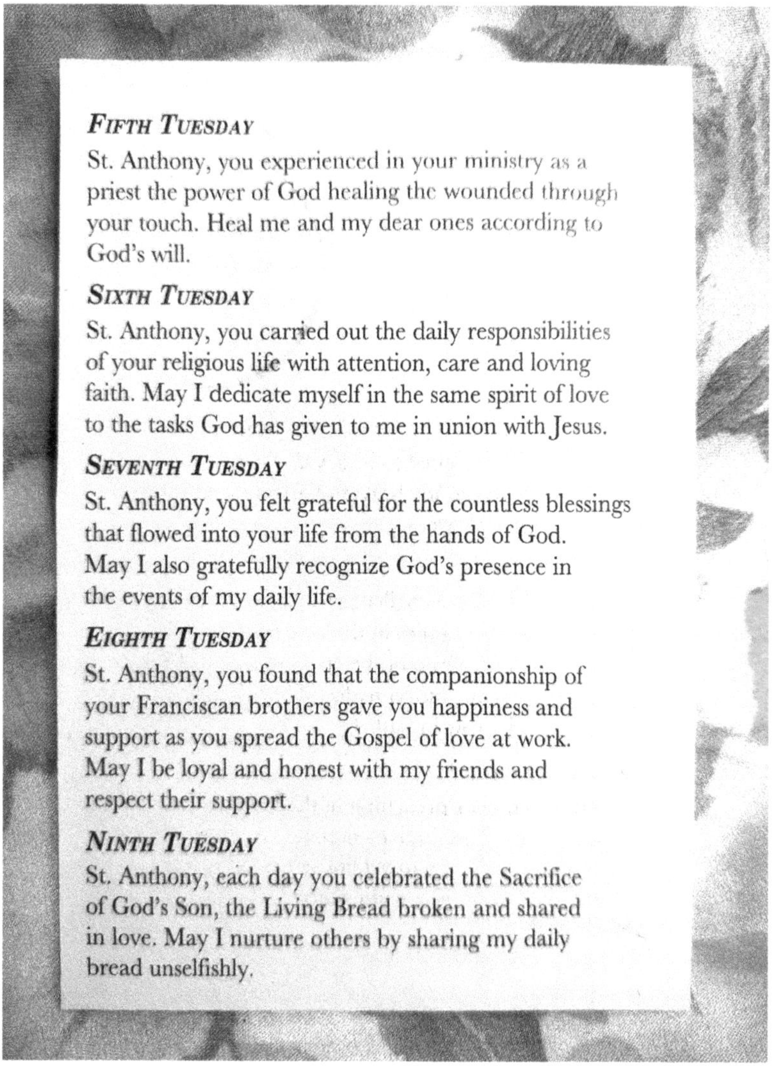

FIFTH TUESDAY
St. Anthony, you experienced in your ministry as a priest the power of God healing the wounded through your touch. Heal me and my dear ones according to God's will.

SIXTH TUESDAY
St. Anthony, you carried out the daily responsibilities of your religious life with attention, care and loving faith. May I dedicate myself in the same spirit of love to the tasks God has given to me in union with Jesus.

SEVENTH TUESDAY
St. Anthony, you felt grateful for the countless blessings that flowed into your life from the hands of God. May I also gratefully recognize God's presence in the events of my daily life.

EIGHTH TUESDAY
St. Anthony, you found that the companionship of your Franciscan brothers gave you happiness and support as you spread the Gospel of love at work. May I be loyal and honest with my friends and respect their support.

NINTH TUESDAY
St. Anthony, each day you celebrated the Sacrifice of God's Son, the Living Bread broken and shared in love. May I nurture others by sharing my daily bread unselfishly.

Figure 16.

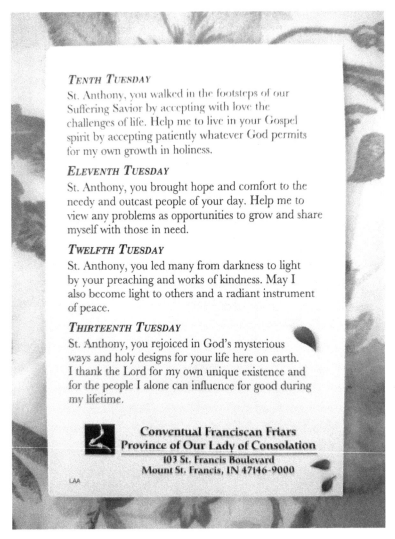

TENTH TUESDAY

St. Anthony, you walked in the footsteps of our Suffering Savior by accepting with love the challenges of life. Help me to live in your Gospel spirit by accepting patiently whatever God permits for my own growth in holiness.

ELEVENTH TUESDAY

St. Anthony, you brought hope and comfort to the needy and outcast people of your day. Help me to view any problems as opportunities to grow and share myself with those in need.

TWELFTH TUESDAY

St. Anthony, you led many from darkness to light by your preaching and works of kindness. May I also become light to others and a radiant instrument of peace.

THIRTEENTH TUESDAY

St. Anthony, you rejoiced in God's mysterious ways and holy designs for your life here on earth. I thank the Lord for my own unique existence and for the people I alone can influence for good during my lifetime.

Conventual Franciscan Friars
Province of Our Lady of Consolation
103 St. Francis Boulevard
Mount St. Francis, IN 47146-9000

LAA

Figure 17.

OPEN TO POSSIBILITIES

REV. ROBERT J. GRECCO

I think making novenas is a good discipline. It shows a lot of trust. But, we sometimes feel like we're going to control God by saying this prayer over nine days. "You *must* do what I want because I followed the prescriptions." That's not openness, you know?

But when it comes to Saint Anthony finding things for us, yes, that's a set outcome, but you know what? Often that has nothing to do with salvation either. We just lost something. It has no bearing on our souls.

But when we're praying otherwise, we have to be *open* to what God determines is best for us. It is not only what's going to work in *this* world, but what's going to help us to then gain eternal happiness. *That's* the goal.

LORRAINE

I don't pray to Saint Anthony all the time. I have another little prayer I say, "Jesus lost, Jesus found." And I'm still saying it.

It was a nice day in November and I love going to the zoo, but I wasn't sure how to drive there. So I took the Greentree bus into town and picked up the 71B Highland, and I rode to the end of the line near the zoo, then walked to the gate.

For some reason, I don't think it was terribly cold that day, but I decided to take my very good, favorite pair of black Isotoner gloves. Well, lo and behold, at the end of my day trip when I got off the bus, I was the last passenger, and I left them on the seat. I only realized it when I was walking from the bus stop and it pulled away. So I sort of tried to catch the bus— which was ridiculous! And that was it.

So when I got home that day I called Port Authority. They said no one had turned them in, but for me to keep on checking from time to time, which I have been doing since the end of November. And I'm *still* thinking one of these days I'm going to get them back.

I also have thought, you know, maybe the person who found them really *needed* them, and I have two or three pairs of other gloves. So then I said, thinking about that person, "I'm happy you found them."

And I decided that if the gloves *should* turn up, I will give them to a person that I see downtown. I see people downtown that look not too prosperous. So I could do that, even though I like the gloves and they're special to me.

MARY Y.

My nursing pin that I lost, I have been invoking Saint Anthony, and it's been several years now. But still I am very much hopeful that I will find it.

This pin for me is my nursing career. And *that* was my life as I know it and as I've lived it from 1961. And wearing that through my whole career, my whole life. It's like, you know, a piece of me that I want to find.

It was lost once before, and with Saint Anthony's help I found it. It was in the laundry. I found it on a piece of clothing in the laundry basket. The pin is about an inch in diameter. The front has "St. Francis School of Nursing 1961." It's gold. And on the back it has my initials before I was married. It's a clip-on pin, you know.

Yes, I am still very hopeful, and sometimes I will start through the house again. The last time I wore it, I think it was to one of my nursing group functions, which was several years ago. And my memory comes back to removing it from my coat and putting it in a pocket somewhere.

So I went on a hunt, and I couldn't stop hunting, because I spent twenty-four hours a day hunting. Then I gave it up, but I go back periodically. And when you came and asked me about the project I thought, "Well, I'll start again." Of course, I always begin with prayer.

Saint Anthony was a gentle person. He was a kind man. And I admired *how* he lived. I admire the saints. I have so much respect for the fact that they lived their lives *that* way, that he lived his life the way *he* did with prayer. He gave up so much and sacrificed and prayed for *othe*r people. In *this* day and age, we are busy *living*.

Yes, and Saint Francis was our patron saint of nursing. I have always kept the "Prayer of Saint Francis" prayer card that was given to us when we were capped. But I don't know a whole lot about his life. He was kind to others, helped the poor and was a lover of animals.

But I'm glad you invited me to speak to you about Saint Anthony because now, I'm going to start again and see if I can, with his direction, find my nursing pin. Because the pin is a treasure to me. To hold that pin would really tell so much about me, you know, in my journey through life, and I hope I can find it.

JOANN C.

I know my parents prayed to Saint Anthony, but I credit my faithful brother with teaching me the rhyming prayer. He and I passed along this belief to ninety-nine percent of the time to find misplaced items—the usual credit cards, cell phone, and many other items.

But there is a more valuable object that has been missing for some time now. I am continuing to pray to Saint Anthony, and I have faith that one day I will find it.

When my mother was in her early nineties, some family and friends got together and pitched in for a special birthday gift, to show appreciation to her for her life of loving and caring and also to acknowledge her strong faith.

I can describe it since I picked it out—a fourteen-karat gold cross one-and-a-quarter inches long, and the chain from which it was suspended was a heavy gold rope chain. She lived with me in those years, and she was very happy with the necklace and very appreciative of such a gift. She wore it every day. It was literally close to her heart.

After she passed, just three months shy of turning ninety-nine, the pain of losing my mother was unbearable. Wearing some of her things was one way of feeling close to her. I remember wearing the cross only a couple of times. Then it went missing. There were workers in and out of my home for various jobs. I don't want to believe someone working in my home would take this. I want to believe it is here somewhere.

Interesting development! When I talked to my brother just days ago, I mentioned this Saint Anthony Oral History Project.

He told me that, a few years ago, after finally retiring, he wanted to devote more time to travel, taking pictures and so on. While visiting Orlando, Florida, he lost his camera.

He attended mass at the Basilica of the National Shrine of Mary, Queen of the Universe.[36] And, marveling at its seventy chapels to the Virgin Mary and the beauty of the architecture and masonry, he mourned the loss of his camera. He shared his plight with the sales woman in the gift shop. She suggested he pray: "Tony, Tony, come around. Something's lost and can't be found." This was something new to him, as he had prayed to the saint, but not with a rhyming prayer like this.

He passed it along to me, but I like to say "Saint Anthony, Saint Anthony, come around, Something's lost and can't be found." That's *my* version because I feel this is more respectful.

My brother left Florida, disappointed that he was leaving behind his Nikon camera and several photos he'd taken. But he continued to pray to Saint Anthony. About two months later, he received a call from the Marriott Hotel where he'd stayed. They found his camera!

They told him their policy for items they find. If lost items are not recovered after two months, the hotel is permitted to check into them. They viewed the pictures in his camera for clues. Some of them he had taken before his retirement. One picture featured a truck with a company name on it and a phone number—my brother's truck, his former company, *his* phone number!

I didn't know the details of this story until he shared with me today. So with new hope, I spent time once again today looking for my mom's cross and praying for a little miracle. And I bless you for sending some prayers my way.

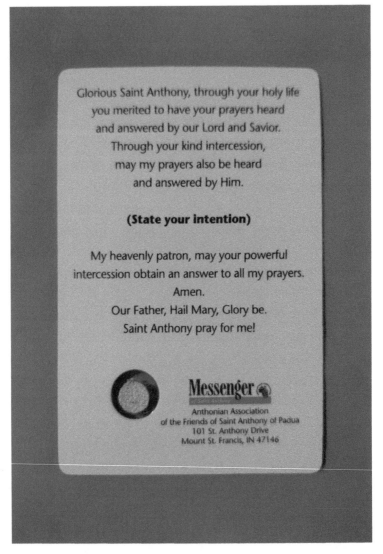

Figure 18.

Part III:

CHRISTMAS IN OUR COMMUNITY

THE CHRISTMAS MESSAGE
THE NATIVITY *SEEN* AND *HERD*

" **D**o not be afraid, Mary, for you have found favor with God. Behold, you will conceive in your womb and bear a son, and you shall name him Jesus. He will be great and will be called Son of the Most High."[37]

> "And so it came to pass that on the solemnity of the Lord's Nativity at Greccio, Francis did something rightly worthy of happy memory so as to represent the infancy of the newborn Savior. During that night in which Christ was born on Earth, he had a crib prepared, hay placed in the crib, and ox and donkey gathered near the crib. The brothers are called from many places to celebrate the solemn vigils. People flock to take in the new mystery and, having obtained torches and candles, make the night bright. The brothers chant the requisite praises to the Lord and the ancient praises of Bethlehem are renewed with a new rite in Greccio. The saint stands before the crib, and he, with Spirit directed toward Heaven, is suffused with ineffable Joy. The

solemnities of the mass are celebrated above the crib and the priest enjoys new consolation."[38]

The above account was written by Thomas of Celano in 1257, describing what took place "on Christmas Eve in 1223... in Greccio, Italy."[39] Francis is "the saint" Celano speaks of, who dramatically presented the scene of the nativity. He had been to the East, to Bethlehem. His rendition used just the two named animals and a carved image of the baby lying on a crevice in a large stone, the manger softened with hay.[40]

Celano tells us that the brothers were called from many places. Anthony was a member of the Order and had already begun to preach in the north, and it is unknown whether he made the journey at that time to central Italy. But he certainly preached inspiring sermons at Christmas. As Franciscan friar Jack Wintz points out, "In Anthony's sermons, especially those on the Incarnation, he uses the image of a powerful God coming down to us...where the king is wrapped in swaddling clothes and lying in a manger."[41]

A CHRISTMAS ALBUM

Figure 19.

Figure 20.

Figure 21.

Figure 22.

Figure 23.

Figure 24.

Figure 25.

Figure 26.

Figure 27.

The End

Epilogue

MODERN-DAY MIRACLE

D uring the Coronavirus response, in March the Diocese of Pittsburgh joined in the worldwide effort to reduce the number of cases by suspending public celebration of the Mass. Sometime before this, I was in church when I heard an extraordinary witness.

I want to respect the privacy of the people involved, so it is not possible for me to disclose greater detail. Three individuals traveled to a Marian shrine, one of whom had been suffering from an ailment. The three were submerged in blessed waters. Two came out sopping wet as one would expect, but everyone was amazed that the third emerged completely dry!! The two friends believed that their traveling companion had received a miracle, with good health for many years.

Hearing this was stunning. Immediately, I thought of one of the miracles attributed to then Blessed Anthony in the 1232 Assiduous collection, miracle #49 (XLIX) entitled "Concerning The Woman Who Threw Herself Into A River But Remained Dry." Of all the miracles recounted, this is one of the longest, going into detail to explain motivations and so on. The story describes a married woman's struggles with her husband, and here is an excerpt:

> "…the sad woman, when all hope was taken away from her and her trust was completely rendered vain, gave in to her self-destructiveness and, invoking the name of blessed Anthony, threw herself into the river which flowed along the road. When the other women who were present saw her being tossed about in the midst of the flowing river, they were initially made breathless by the shock, but then hastened to her as quickly as possible…getting themselves wet up to their waist lines with all their garments, they pulled her out of the water that had covered her completely. When she was pulled out, and they had placed her along the bank— I narrate what is truly marvelous! It was found that not even a thread of her undergarment was wet, whereas the women who had saved her were wringing out their clothes to force the excessive quantity of water out of them."[42]

While I can understand that some believers question the possibility of miracles, and I have read that even religious writers call attention to embellishment of legends told of Saint Anthony through the course of time, I can't help but connect the story alluded to above with the event that was described in Italy nearly 800 years ago.

And, having experienced some unusual occurrences in my own life, I am comfortable in believing that I receive help from God through the saints. The process of writing this book has led me to not only embrace the possibility of modern-day miracles, but to recognize that these can, and still do happen, if we remain prayerfully open to possibilities, and…if we ask!

On another note, I often wonder at the powerful sign I received in the medical center last fall. I am curious about "Anthony of the Lobby." What brought him there? I returned in January for a follow-up, after my European trip. My feet were fine. My prime reason for going was to ask about *him* at the reception desk. Could it be that he is an employee? Of course privacy policies prevent me from knowing. But I carried the CGS bulletin ad, described the project, and left a copy with the receptionist. It's probably long gone, but in any case, I want to thank him.

Wherever you are—Anthony, Antonio, Antoine—thank *you* for helping to set me on this course, discovering Saint Anthony.

POSTSCRIPT

Thank you for joining us!
Come along on a great European adventure in my next book:

Discovering Saint Anthony: Portugal to Padua

TABLE OF FIGURES

1. The Miraculous Responsory by Julian of Speyer (d.1250, Paris, France) Composed 1233/1234.

2. Pen and Ink drawing, card commissioned by Aleksandr Joseph Schrenk for his priestly ordination at St. Paul Cathedral, Pittsburgh, PA. June 24, 2017.

3. Copper plaque embossed with the image of St. Anthony, photo shared by Louise Marino.

4. "A Prayer of Petition"

> O Wondrous Saint Anthony, holy and learned in the things of God because you had drunk so deeply of His Word in the Scriptures: teach me the answers to the problems of Life. Intercede in my behalf for the favor that I desire so much. I know I have failed many times in the past; I did not respond to your call to love and be holy. But I never turned away from you; for this reason, turn toward me in my need. I promise to make tomorrow better: to love my family more deeply and truly, to serve my brothers and sisters with greater generosity, and to

be devoted to the service of the poor. Strengthen
my resolution and obtain for me the grace to die in
the love of God.
Amen.

#648 ST. ANTHONY'S GUILD, PATERSON, NJ. (printed
with permission)

5. "A Prayer of Thanksgiving"

O GLORIOUS wonder-worker, Saint Anthony,
father of the poor and comforter of the Afflicted,
thou who hast come with such loving solicitude
to my assistance, and hast comforted me so abundantly behold me at thy feet to offer thee my heart-
felt thanks. Accept, therefore, this offering and
with it my earnest promise which I now renew, to
live Always in the love of Jesus and my neighbor.
Continue to shield me graciously with thy Protection,
and obtain for me the final grace of being able one
day to enter the kingdom Of heaven, there to sing
with thee the everlasting mercies of God. Amen.

Indulgence of 300 days, once a day; plenary indulgence,
on the usual conditions, if recited daily for a month
(S.P.Ap., March 4, 1933).

#593 ST. ANTHONY'S GUILD, PATERSON, NJ. (printed
with permission)

6. Molly, a terrier mix, wearing St. Anthony/St. Francis pet medal.

7. St. Anthony/St. Francis pet medal,
    purchased at JMJ Catholic Bookstore, Bethel Park, PA.

8. San Damiano cross.

9. Tau cross on chain.

10. Vial of blessed oil
The Shrine of St. Anthony
Ellicott City, MD.

11. Ethereal print of Saint Anthony with Infant Jesus
205 Johnson Gordon Co., Chicago, IL.

12. Scapular from Lourdes, France.

13. Rosary from Lourdes, France.

14. One-decade loop rosary with Saint Anthony medal.

Franciscan Friars of the Atonement
Garrison, New York 10524
(845) 424-2138
www.AtonementFriars.org

15. Novena from the Conventual Franciscan Friars:
Short Prayers for "Thirteen Tuesdays"
First Tuesday–Fourth Tuesday.

16. Novena prayers, (contd.): Fifth Tuesday–Ninth Tuesday.

17. Novena prayers (contd.): Tenth
Tuesday–Thirteenth Tuesday.

Conventual Franciscan Friars
Province of Our Lady of Consolation
103 St. Francis Boulevard
Mount St. Francis, IN 47146.

18. "St. Anthony, Pray for Us" prayer card, back.

This holy piece of cloth has been blessed through physical contact with Saint Anthony's Tongue at his Basilica in Padua, Italy.

Messenger of Saint Anthony
Anthonian Association of the Friends of Saint Anthony of Padua
101 St. Anthony Drive
Mount St. Francis, IN 47146

The above is an old address. The new address is:
6107 N. Kenmore Ave., Ste. 5
Chicago, IL 60660

19. Nativity scene at Saint Elizabeth Ann Seton Church, 2019.

20. Nativity scene at Saint Elizabeth Ann Seton Church, 2019.

21. Nativity scene at Saint Elizabeth Ann Seton Church, 2019.

22. Nativity scene at Saint Margaret of Scotland Church, 2019.

23. Nativity scene at Saint Margaret of Scotland Church, 2019.

24. Nativity scene at Saint Margaret of Scotland School, 2019.

25. Nativity celebrated by SS. Simon & Jude Church.

26. Nativity celebrated by SS. Simon & Jude Early Childhood Center, 2019.

27. Nativity celebrated by SS. Simon & Jude Early Childhood Center, 2019.

Front cover-devotional area at St. Elizabeth Ann Seton Church.

The single-strand, one-decade rosary used as a recurring design was recently given to the author, and no other information is available.

NOTES

1. Vergilio Gamboso, ed. *Life of St Anthony: Assidua*. Translated by Bernard Przewozny, (Padova: Messaggero, 2019), 5.

2. Gamboso, ed., "Here Begin the Miracles of Blessed Anthony" in *Assidua*, 67-95.

3. Michael E. Gaitley, *33 Days to Morning Glory*, (Stockbridge Mass.:Marian Press, 2015).

4. Michael E. Gaitley, *Consoling the Heart of Jesus*, (Sycamore, Illinois:Lighthouse Catholic Media, 2010).

5. Grzegorz Górny. *Guadalupe Mysteries: deciphering the code*, (San Francisco:Ignatius Press, 2016).

6. *We Knew What We Had: The Greatest Jazz Story Never Told,* YouTube video, 1:12.Posted by MCGJazz.Feb 2, 2018.https:// www.youtube.com/watch?v=JUs5tovT7EQ(accessed March 25, 2020).

7. *Singing in the Rain*, Directed by Gene Kelly and Stanley Donen. Culver California: MGM, 1952.

8. Saint Augustine (of Hippo), *The Confessions of S. Augustine*, (London:J. Parker & Co.,1868).

9. Basilica Pontificia di Sant'Antonio di Padova (Basilica of Saint Anthony of Padua), is the site where the body of St. Anthony is entombed and his relics are venerated. In the days and weeks following Anthony's funeral, the number of miracles occurring at his tomb helped make a strong case for his canonization, and this took place less than a year after his death, June 13,1231. First entombed in his small friary, after the construction of a basilica encompassing that space, his tomb was moved, and it has been moved additional times over the years with various structural modifications and enhancements to the basilica. The breathtaking side altar was begun in 1500 and completed towards the end of that century. Via a live webcam at the site, St. Anthony's tomb can be viewed 24 hours a day. "Saint Anthony of Padua," Messaggero di S.Antonio Editrice, 2020, (March 8, 2020).https://www.santantonio.org/en.

According to Maria Hart, the Director of the Anthonian Association in the U.S., this is a worldwide non-profit and charitable organization. The O.F.M. Conventuals of the basilica are responsible for the monthly publication, *The Messenger of Saint Anthony* which has worldwide distribution, now in 35 countries. Subscription to the magazine is available through the above website. Telephone conversation March 25, 2020.

10. Padre Giuseppe Abate (1889-1969) Franciscan friar. Gamboso, *Life of Saint Anthony*, 141.

11. Vergilio Gamboso, *Life of Saint Anthony*. Translated by. H. Partridge. (Padua, Italy: EMP, 1979), 90-91.

12. Matt. 7:7-8 (NAB).

13. Saint Anthony Chapel, 1704 Harpster Street, Pittsburgh, Pa 15212, (412) 323-9504. Construction of the devotional chapel was completed in 1883, and the dedication of the chapel took place on June 13, Anthony's feast day. The annex was completed in 1892. The Thirteen Tuesday Novena in honor of St. Anthony of Padua is conducted every year, scheduled to conclude on June 13. The chapel contains over five thousand relics of saints, reputedly "the most venerated relic," a tooth of St. Anthony. The chapel has been designated a Historical Landmark by the Pittsburgh History and Landmarks Foundation. "Saint Anthony Chapel," e-Catholic, (accessed Feb 25, 2020), https://stanthonyschapel.org/the-chapel.

14. In the summer of 1220, Fernando left the Santa Cruz monastery of the Augustinians in Coimbra, Portugal to join the Franciscans. He put off the white robe and donned "the poor habit of the Friars Minor," wanting to go on a mission to preach in Morocco and hoping to become a martyr for Christ. Fernando took a new name, the name of the patron saint of the small friary nearby that was surrounded by olive trees, Santo António dos Olivais. Sophronius Clasen, *St. Anthony: Doctor of the Church*, translated by Ignatius Brady, (Chicago: Franciscan Herald Press, 1973), 15-17.

15. KofC contributed more than $185 million to charity and donated more than 76 million hours of service in the U.S. and abroad to mentioned programs as well as Coats for Kids, Christian Refugee Relief, and Disaster Relief. "Knights of Columbus," 2020, (accessed March 6, 2020), https://www.kofc.org/.

According to Gary Williard, KofC member of St. Elizabeth Ann Seton Council #11143, the council is the joint effort of this community. Cards are sent to shut-ins, and they hold Bingo monthly for residents in nursing homes. They coordinate activities for Divine Mercy Sunday. Numerous team projects include manning festival booths and holding pancake breakfasts. Members sell lottery calendars and COAL tickets, and their annual Tootsie Roll Drive raises funds for the council and for local organizations such as St. Anthony School Programs and McGuire Home. The Baby Bottle Campaign is a local outreach to support mothers in need.

In support of life, the Rosary is prayed outside some places where abortions are likely to occur. Our local has vans fitted with ultrasound machines that save lives, "helping women choose life...giving them the opportunity to view their unborn children. Once the expectant mothers see their babies, over 80% carry their babies full term."
"Knights of Columbus," 2020, (accessed March 6, 2020), https://www.kofc.org/en/what-we-do/faith-in-action-programs/life/ultrasound-program.html.

16. Matt. 7:21 and Matt. 25:31-46 (NAB).

17. Matt. 25:23 "Come, share your master's joy!"

18. St. Anthony School Programs serve a 4-county area, providing educational programs for children of all faiths who are challenged with Down Syndrome, Autism Spectrum Disorder and Intellectual Disabilities. Allegheny County site: 2000 Corporate Dr. #580, Wexford, Pa.15090, (844) 782-5437. In the South Hills, St. Thomas More Catholic School integrates the St. Anthony School Program into its

student body for children ages K-8. "St. Anthony School Programs," 2017, (accessed Feb 8, 2020), https://www. stanthonykids.org/.

19. According to Fr. Jerome, The Guild of St. Anthony is a pious society, a lay organization. It was founded in Nigeria by missionary priests in 1920 as part of the modern Catholic mission, when various lay organizations emerged. The Guild of St. Anthony is not to be confused with St. Anthony's Guild, a fundraising organization guided by the Franciscan Friars. Holy Name Province, 144 West 32nd St., New York, NY 10001 (212) 564-8799. "St. Anthony's Guild: Home" (accessed March 9, 2020),https://stanthonysguild.org/.

St. Anthony's Guild was founded in the U.S. in 1924 by John Forrest Loviner, (Order of Friars Minor) who had been born on the feast day of St. Anthony of Padua in 1896 in Columbus, Ohio. A year after Loviner's ordination, working from the Bonaventure Friary in Paterson, New Jersey, he purchased a building there and in 1927 began publication of The Anthonian. The guild print shop, which opened in 1930, became one of the largest producers of catechetical literature in the U.S. (Figures 4 and 5 are samples.)
"John Forest Loviner" (accessed March 9, 2020), https:// st.anthonysguild./hnp-friars/john-forest-loviner.
Jocelyn Thomas, "St. Anthony's Guild Plans 90th Anniversary Celebration," *Around the Province*, (accessed March 5, 2014), https://hnp.org/communications/ articles-and-speeches/.

20.This beautiful story resembles a traditional Italian narrative recounted by Stoddard, Saint Anthony portrayed as a protector of children: The mother sees her child fall from a high window, and she cries to Anthony for help. As she rushes to her son, he runs to her and says, "A friar caught me in his arms and placed me gently on the ground." The mother then takes her child to offer thanks at Ara Coeli, the old Franciscan church in Rome. Upon entering the church, the little boy points to a picture and says, "See, there is the friar who saved me!" The pictured saint was Anthony of Padua. Charles Warren Stoddard, "The Glories of Anthony" in *Saint Anthony: The Wonder-Worker of Padua*, ed. (Charlotte, N.C., TAN Books, 1978) 97-98.

21. The term *Franciscan* traces from St. Francis of Assisi (b.1181/1182–October 3,1226)."Francis insolently followed the early teaching of his parents right up to the twenty-fifth year of his life, squandered his time vainly, practice of vanities and revelry...One day the Lord revealed to him in prayer what he needed to do...truly held riches in contempt and despised money. He went among the lepers... kissed them...and cleansing the pus from their sores...He began to preach penance to everyone, granted in simple words, but with a magnificent heart. He began by saying, as the Lord had revealed to him, 'May the Lord give you peace.'" Thomas of Celano. *The Rediscovered Life of St. Francis of Assisi*, ed. Jacques Dalarun and trans. Timothy J. Johnson (St. Bonaventure University: Franciscan Institute Publications, 2016), 2-6.

"The foundation of the Poor Ladies or Second Order" of Franciscans "may be said to have been laid in 1212. In that year St. Clare who had besought St. Francis to be allowed to embrace the new manner of life he had instituted, was established by him at St. Damian's near Assisi, together with several other pious maidens who had joined her."

Francis did not "draw up a formal rule for these Poor ladies and no mention of such a document is found in any of the early authorities. The rule imposed upon the Poor Ladies at St. Damian's about 1219 by Cardinal Ugolino, afterwards Gregory IX, was recast by St. Clare towards the end of her life, with the assistance of Cardinal Rinaldo, afterwards Alexander IV, and in this revised form was approved by Innocent IV, 9 Aug., 1253 (Litt. "Solet Annuere")." "Franciscan Order" 2017, (accessed March 5, 2020), https://www.newadvent.org/cathen/06217a.htm.

The Poor Ladies' followers became known as the Poor Clares, and continue their mission today, as do many incarnations of this ideal. Locally, the Sisters of St. Francis of the Providence of God "have provided a child-centered environment for children for 35 years" at The Franciscan Child Day Care Center in Whitehall. Their mission, "Childcare is in our Hearts and Children are the Heart of our Center," is "inspired by Francis of Assisi to follow Jesus Christ in total responsiveness to the Providence of God... and to proclaim peace in the joy of the spirit." "Sisters of St. Francis of the Providence of God," 2020, (accessed March 5, 2020), www.franciscanchilddaycare.org.

22. This is the "Unfailing Prayer to St. Anthony." The prayer begins: "Blessed be God in His Angels and in His Saints." "Unfailing Prayer to St. Anthony" (accessed March 8, 2020)https://www.catholic.org/prayers/prayer.php?=163. The original prayer card was obtained from Franciscan Friars of the Atonement at Graymoor, 40 Franciscan Way, Garrison, NY, 10524. (888) 720-8247. Graymoor has acquired from Assisi the altar where St. Francis received his holy stigmata on Mt. Alverna in 1224, now located

there in the St. Francis Chapel. According to Director of Communications Jonathon Hotz, there is a statue of St. Francis of Assisi above the altar which is one of only two made from a mold of Francis' death mask (the other is in Assisi). At the left side of the altar is a statue of St. Anthony, and this is where Father Paul Wattson, S.A. and the Friars began their perpetual novena to St. Anthony in 1912. (accessed March 7, 2020), https://www.atonementfriars.org/graymoor-holy-mountain/#st_francis_chapel.

Anthony's true likeness can be seen on the front cover of Spilsbury's recent volume. The impressive "bust in bronze" by Roberto Cremesini, sculpted in 1995, was obtained through "forensic reconstruction derived from the measurements of the Saint's skull" when the body was exhumed in 1981. The results of radiographic analysis of the bones suggest that he lived longer than previously thought. The traditional birth date, 1195, is modified to circa 1191, so he lived approximately 40 years. Paul Spilsbury, *Saint Anthony of Padua: His Life and Writings*, 2nd Reprint (P.P.F.M.C. Messaggero Di Sant'Antonio-Editrice, 2015), front cover, 33.

23. Secular Franciscans are also referred to as lay Franciscans, a branch of the Franciscan Family formed by lay Catholic men and women who seek to observe the Gospel of Jesus by following the example of St. Francis of Assisi. "Secular Franciscan Order–USA," 2020, (accessed March 7, 2020), secularfranciscansusa.org.

The Secular Franciscan Order (Ordo Franciscanus Saecularis), also known as the Third Order, was "founded by Francis about 1221 calls devout persons...living in the world and following a rule of life approved by Nicholas IV in 1289, and modified by Leo XIII, 30 May, 1883" (Constit. "Misericors"). "Franciscan Order" 2017, (accessed March 7, 2020), www.newadvent.org/cathen/06217a.htm.

24. The San Damiano (Saint Damian) cross is that cross before which Francis prayed in the Assisi church he would rebuild, early in his conversion. Bonaventure wrote a biography of Francis in 1263 which tells how this came about: "For one day when Francis went out to meditate in the fields, he walked near the church of San Damiano which was threatening to collapse because of age. Impelled by the Spirit, he went inside to pray. Prostrate before an image of the Crucified, he was filled with no little consolation as he prayed. While his tear-filled eyes were gazing at the Lord's cross, he heard with his bodily ears a voice coming from that cross, telling him three times: "Francis, go and repair my house which, as you see, is all being destroyed."

Trembling, Francis was stunned at the sound of such an astonishing voice, since he was alone in the church; and as he absorbed the power of the divine words into his heart, he fell into an ecstasy of mind. At last, coming back to himself, he prepared himself to obey and pulled himself together to carry out the command of repairing the material church, although the principal intention of the words referred to *that which Christ purchased with his own blood…"*
"His Perfect Conversion to God and His Repair of 3 Churches," Regis Armstrong, Wayne Hellmann, and William J Short, eds. Vol.2, 1999-2001. Franciscan Intellectual Tradition. *The Life of Blessed Francis*: FA:ED, vol. 2, p. 536. (accessed March 23, 2020) https://www.franciscantradition.org/francis-of-assisi-early-documents/the-founder/the-legends-and-sermons-

about-saint-francis-by-bonaventure-of-bagnoregio/
the-major-legend-of-saint-francis/the-life-of-blessed-
francis/1625-fa-ed-2-page-536#ges:searchword=san+dam
iano+cross&searchphrase=all&page=1.

The Tau cross is also of great significance. Tau is the upper-case form of the letter *T* in the Greek alphabet, and there is a reference in the Old Testament Book of Ezekiel to its use among penitents: "This conviction should be faithfully and devotedly in the forefront of our minds: not only does this advance the mission he held of calling to weep and mourn, {snippet Is 22:12} to shave one's head and wear sackcloth, and to sign the Tau{snippet Ez 9:4} on the foreheads of those moaning and grieving with a sign of a penitential cross, and of a habit conformed to the cross...."

Prologue, Regis Armstrong, O.F.M. Cap., Wayne Hellmann, O.F.M. Conv., and William J. Short., eds.Vol. 2,1999-2001. The Life of Blessed Francis: FA:ED, vol. 2, p. 527 (March 23, 2020)

https://www.franciscantradition.org/francis-of-assisi-
early-documents/the-founder/the-legends-and-sermons-
about-saint-francis-by-bonaventure-of-bagnoregio/
the-major-legend-of-saint-francis/the-life-of-blessed-
francis/1616-fa-ed-2-page-527#ges:searchword%3Dtau%
2Bcross%26searchphrase%3Dall%26page%3D1.

"St. Francis used the Tau in his writings, and even used it as his signature."
"Friar's E-spirations:The Franciscan Coat of Arms" (accessed April 22,2020)
https://www.franciscanmedia.org/friar-s-e-spirations-
the-franciscan-coat-of-arms/.

25.The Shrine of St. Anthony, in Ellicott City, Maryland 21042, is a ministry of the Franciscan Friars Conventual, a branch of the order founded for men by Francis of Assisi in 1209. (accessed March 18, 2020) https://www.merriam-webster.com/dictionary/conventual. (accessed Feb 26, 2020) "The Shrine of St. Anthony"http://ShrineofStAnthony.org.

The Gospel life of the Friars Minor today has "four central components: 1. to be men of prayer, 2 .to live as lesser ones, 3. to create a brotherhood of mutual care among ourselves, and 4. to go about the world as heralds of God's reign and agents of Gospel peace." "USFranciscans" accessed March 5, 2020.accessed March 5, 2020.
https://usfranciscans.org.

In our modern world, these charisms translate to the 3 branches of the First order, each containing all 4 components but with varied focus. One way of looking at the differences is the way the Conventuals live in a "convent," in brotherhood and community; Capuchins in prayer and contemplation with greater solitude; and Friars Minor make up a larger population, seeking involvement in the apostolate of active ministry.

Biographers of Anthony have provided many examples of how he fulfilled his ministry with holiness and excellence in each area. Sophronius Clasen, for instance, makes the point that, "in a happy balance of the apostolate and the life of solitude, he surrendered himself after the example of saints to the all-wise guidance of God.
Clasen, *St. Anthony:Doctor of the Church*, 63.

Vergilio Gamboso describes Anthony's standing in the Order just after Francis' death: "At the Chapter meeting of

1227, Anthony had already "made a well-deserved name for himself in propagating the Order in France and was highly respected for his intellectual gifts and holy lifestyle. He was chosen as Provincial Minister of Emilia, a vast, densely populated area in Northern Italy...and embroiled in heresy and conflict." He "governed his friars with clemency and kindness. He seemed less a Superior than a comrade," and "remained admirably courteous," even though "he surpassed all men in Italy for eloquence and doctrinal knowledge." Gamboso, *Life of Saint Anthony*, 90-91.

26. Sacro Convento di San Francesco d'Assisi (Sacred Convent of Saint Francis) is a Franciscan friary where the mortal remains of St. Francis and those of his first companions have been resting in the basilica. The friars have custody of the body of St. Francis. The website provides a live webcam for 24-hour visitation to the crypt. Basilica di San Francesco d'Assisi (accessed March 9, 2020) https://www.sanfrancescoassisi.org.

27. Companions of St. Anthony is a mission for the advancement and development of the Franciscan friars of the province, The Holy Name Province. Primarily the funds are for their education and for support of the Shrine of St. Anthony in Ellicott City, Md. "Companions of St. Anthony" (accessed Feb 18, 2020), https//www.companionsofstanthony.org.

28. Holy Land Treasures USA offers hand-carved olivewood creations. According to the information on the website, many of the olive trees are supplied from the Galilee region, the wood carved by a local artisan at their factory on Manger Street in Bethlehem, Palestine. The finished piece comes with a certificate of authenticity, "Made in the Holy Land."

In the U.S., their gift shop is located in Wake County, North Carolina. "Holy Land Treasures" (accessed Feb 18, 2020) https://www.holylandtreasuresonline.com.

29. Saint Louis-Marie Grignion de Montfort (1673-1716), was a French priest and Confessor as well as an early writer in the field of Mariology. Known in his time for his devotion to the Blessed Virgin Mary and the practice of saying the Rosary, he was a charismatic preacher who combated heresy and ministered to soldiers. There is a story from La Rochelle, France of him ministering to "soldiers who were so moved by his words, they wept and cried for the forgiveness of their sins. In the procession which terminated this mission, an officer walked at the head, barefooted and carrying a banner, and the soldiers also barefooted, carrying in one hand a crucifix, in the other a rosary, and singing hymns."(accessed March 4, 2020) "St. Louis de Montfort," http://www.newadvent.org/cathen/09384a.htm.

30. Eternal Word Television Network is an American-based cable television network that broadcasts round-the-clock Catholic themed programming. It was founded in 1981 by Mother Mary Angelica (b.1923, Canton, Ohio, d. 2016, Hanceville, Alabama), a member of the cloistered nuns, the Poor Clares. (March 11, 2020)https://www.ewtn.com.

The EWTN staff of Franciscan friars "come from around the country and around the world." Some familiar faces to the television audience include Fr. Joseph Mary, Fr. Mark Mary, Fr. John Paul Mary, and Br. John Therese Marie. "The Friars"(March 11, 2020) https://franciscanmissionaries. com/the-friars/.

The upbeat *ICONS* features young twin Franciscan Friars of the Renewal, Fr. Innocent Montgomery and Fr. Angelus Montgomery as well as Fr. Augustino Torres. "Icons," (accessed March 11, 2020) https://www.ewtn.com/tv/shows/icons.

31. According to parishioner Rajkumar Manoharan who is a native of Chennai, Tamilnadu, India, the indigenous Thamizh (Tamil) dialect spoken in this southern region has multiple pronunciations for the British English digraph /th/. So that spelling may be pronounced either AN-tho-nee or AN-to-nee.

32. (Luke 18: 1-8) NAB

33. St. Bonaventure (1221-1274) was born in Italy during the time of Francis of Assisi, and the traditional story is that he received this name as a result of an exclamation of Francis when the child's mother pleaded with him to pray for her little son who was very ill. Francis' gifts allowed him to foresee a great future for this child, and so Francis exclaimed, "O buona ventura!"(O good fortune) Indeed the boy would grow up healthy, and when he was twenty-two he entered the Franciscan Order. "St. Bonaventure" (March 8, 2020),http://www.newadvent.org/cathen/02648c.htm.

"In 1263, the new Basilica of St. Anthony was completed, and his remains were re-interred in a more magnificent tomb on the Octave of Easter." By this time, Bonaventure was Minister General of the Franciscans, and so he presided. When the Saint's remains were disinterred, it was found that his tongue was incorrupt, as red and soft as it had been thirty and more years before. St. Bonaventure took it into his hands and venerated it: "O blessed tongue which ever blessed the Lord and made others bless him! Now

it is abundantly clear how much you merited from God."
"This event was widely reported, and gave fresh impetus
to the Anthonian cultus." Paul Spilsbury, *Saint Anthony of
Padua: His Life and Writings*, 2nd Reprint (Messaggero Di
Sant'Antonio-Editrice, 2015),140.

34. St. Vincent de Paul Society was founded in Paris in 1833 to
help the people living in slums. Today the organization is
a registered non-profit whose lay Catholic members, called
"Vincentians," seek personal holiness through works of
charity. The society's mission is to live the gospel message
by serving Christ in the poor with love, respect, hope, and
joy, and by working to shape a more just and compassionate
society. They accept donations for the operation of several
thrift stores and food banks to benefit the poor and needy.
Our Catholic community helpline is (412) 444-5425. "Society
of St. Vincent De Paul" (accessed March 8, 2020) http://
svdppitt.org.

35. St. Anthony Mission Partner-My Mass Request-Seraphic
Mass Association & Capuchin Mission Office, 5217 Butler
Street, suite 100, Pittsburgh Pa, 15201. (877)737-9050.
(accessed March 10, 2020) "Become a St. Anthony Mission
Partner," https://mymassrequest.org/Ways-to-Give/
St-Anthony-Mission-Partners/Join.

36. Basilica of the National Shrine of Mary, Queen of the
Universe is at 8300 Vineland Ave., Orlando, Florida.
32821. Construction began on December 8, 1984.The
construction of the massive, expertly crafted pipe organ
consisting of 5,271 pipes, will be completed in November,
2020. "Basilica of the National Shrine of Mary, Queen of

the Universe," (accessed March 12, 2020) https://www.maryqueenoftheuniverse.org.

When Saint Anthony was to be baptized, his parents had only to walk across the street from their home to Sé, the grand, new Romanesque cathedral named Santa Maria Maior de Lisboa (St. Mary Major of Lisbon). He attended school there and, by all accounts, was devoted to the Blessed Mother throughout his life.

Sophronius Clasen, O.F.M. writes of Saint Anthony that "at the sacred font he received the name Ferdinand (Fernando)." The author refers to his young subject as "Ferdinand." *St. Anthony: Doctor of the Church*, 5-17.

The earliest reference to the infant's given name is "Ferdinand." Gamboso, ed., *Assidua*, 19.

Both versions of the name are used. "Fernando" appears in recent publications by Vergilio Gamboso, O.F.M. Conv., Jack Wintz, O.F.M., and Rev. Dr. Paul Spilsbury, though he refers to the child "already as Anthony."
Gamboso, *Life of Saint Anthony*, 10.
Jack Wintz, *Saint Anthony of Padua:His Life, Legends and Devotions*, (U.S.: St. Anthony Messenger Press, 2012), 11.
Spilsbury, *Saint Anthony of Padua: His Life and Writings*, 33.

On November 1,1755, an earthquake, by today's estimates from 8.5–9 on the moment magnitude scale and a tsunami, destroyed most of Lisbon killing 60,000 people. The cathedral survived however, and extensive repairs, renovations, and modifications have been carried out through the centuries, its upper story now an exhibition of liturgical, devotional and catechism items. Mass is celebrated in the sanctuary.

"Lisbon earthquake of 1755," accessed March 21, 2020) https://www.britannica.com/even/Lisbon-earthquake-of-1755. "Sé Cathedral Lisbon," (accessed March 21, 2020) https://lisbonlisboaportugal.com/Alfama-Lisbon/se-cathedral-lisbon.html.

37. Luke 1:30-32

38. Thomas of Celano, 25.

39. Michael P. Warsaw, *Christmas '19 Family Newsletter*, EWTN Global Catholic Network, Christmas 2019, cover.

40. "Today in Greccio, one can still see the stone—perhaps three feet high and two feet wide—on which the hay was placed...The top has a rough, shallow, V-shaped indentation. Here the carved image of the baby was laid." Jack Wintz, "Saint Francis and the Crib,"Franciscan Media, 2020, (accessed March 22, 2020) https://franciscanmedia.org/saint-francis-and-the-crib/.

41. Jack Wintz, *Saint Anthony of Padua: His Life, Legends, and Devotions*, (U.S.: St. Anthony Messenger Press, 2012), 40-41.

42. Gamboso, ed., *Assidua*, 89-91.

Works Cited

Armstrong, Regis, Wayne Hellmann, and William J. Short, eds. *The Life of Blessed Francis.* "*Francis of Assisi: Early Documents,*" Vol.2, 1999-2001. Franciscan Intellectual Tradition. https//www.franciscantradition.org/.

Clasen, Sophronius. *St. Anthony:Doctor of the Church.* Translated by Ignatius Brady. Chicago:Franciscan Herald Press, 1973. Originally published as Antonius, Diener Des Evangeliums Und Der Kirche (Germany: Kühlen, 1960).

Gaitley, Michael E. *33 Days to Morning Glory: A Do-It-Yourself Retreat in Preparation for Marian Consecration.* Stockbridge, Mass: Marian Press, 2015.

Gamboso, Vergilio. ed. *Life of St Anthony: Assidua.*Translated by Bernard Przewozny, Padova:Messaggero, Reprint 2019.

Gamboso, Vergilio.*Life of Saint Anthony.* Translated by. H. Partridge. Revised by L. Poloniato, 90-91.Reprint, Padua, Italy: 2019.Originally published as La vita di sant'Antonio. Padua, Italy: EMP, 1979.

Górny, Grzegorz. *Guadalupe Mysteries:deciphering the code*. Translated by Stan Kacsprzak, San Francisco: Ignatius Press, 2016.

Saint Augustine (of Hippo). *The Confessions of S. Augustine*. London: J. Parker & Co., 1868.

Spilsbury, Paul. *Saint Anthony of Padua: His Life and Writings*. Padova: Edizioni. Messaggero, 2015.

Stoddard, Charles Warren. "The Glories of Anthony" in *Saint Anthony: The Wonder-Worker of Padua*.Reprint, Charlotte, N.C.: TAN Books, 1978.

Thomas of Celano. *The Rediscovered Life of St. Francis of Assisi*, ed. Jacques Dalarun Translated by Timothy J. Johnson. St. Bonaventure University: Franciscan Institute Publications, 2016.Originally published as Thome Celanensis Vita beati patres sant'Antonio. Padua, Italy: EMP, 1979.

Warsaw, Michael P. *Christmas '19 Family Newsletter*. EWTN Global Catholic Network, 2019.

Wintz, Jack. *Saint Anthony of Padua: His Life, Legends, and Devotions*. U.S.: St. Anthony Messenger Press. 2012.

FILM

Kelly, Gene, Donald O'Connor, and Debbie Reynolds. *Singing in the Rain*. DVD, Directed by Stanley Donen, and Gene Kelly Culver City, California: MGM 1952.

ONLINE RESOURCES

Armstrong, Regis, Wayne Hellmann, and William J Short, eds.

"His Perfect Conversion to God and His Repair of 3 Churches." The Life of Blessed Francis: Vol. 2, p. 536." Franciscan Intellectual Tradition. https://www.franciscantradition. org/francis-of-assisi-early-documents/the-founder/the-legends-and-sermons-about-saint-francis-by-bonaventure-of-bagnoregio/the-major-legend-of-saint-francis/ the-life-of-blessed-francis/1625-fa-ed-2-page-536#ges:sea rchword=san+damiano+cross&searchphrase=all&page=1. (accessed March 23, 2020).

"Assistance." Society of St Vincent de Paul Council of Pittsburgh. https://svdppitt.org/services/assistance/.(accessed March 8, 2020).

"Basilica di San Francesco d'Assisi" https://www. sanfrancescoassisi.org.(accessed March 9, 2020).

"Basilica of the National Shrine of Mary, Queen of the Universe," https://maryqueenoftheuniverse.org/(accessed March 12, 2020).

"Become a St. Anthony Mission Partner," https://mymassrequest. org/Ways-to-Give/St-Anthony-Mission-Partners/Join (accessed March 10, 2020).

"Companions of St. Anthony"https://www.companions ofstanthony.org/(accessed Feb 18, 2020).

EWTN Global Catholic Television Network: Catholic News, TV, Radio. https://www.ewtn.com/. (accessed March 11, 2020).

"The Friars"https://franciscanmissionaries.com/the-friars/. (accessed March 11, 2020).

Friar's E-Spirations: The Franciscan Coat of Arms" https://www. franciscanmedia.org/friar-s-e-spirations-the-franciscan-coat-of-arms/. (accessed April 22, 2020).

"Holy Land Treasures" https://www.holylandtreasuresonline. com(accessed Feb 18, 2020).

"Icons," https://www.ewtn.com/tv/shows/icons(accessed March 11, 2020).

Jamal, Ahmad."We Knew What We Had: The Greatest Jazz Story Never Told."YouTube video, 1:12.Posted by MCGJazz. Feb 2, 2018.https://www.youtube.com/watch?v=JUs5tovT7EQ(accessed March 25. 2020).

"Knights of Columbus," https://www.kofc.org/(accessed March 6, 2020).

"Lisbon Earthquake of 1755"Encyclopaedia Britannica. https://www.britannica.com/event/Lisbon-earthquake-of-1755(accessed March 21, 2020).

Robinson, Paschal. "Franciscan Order." The Catholic Encyclopedia. Vol. 6. New York: Robert Appleton Company, 1909. https://www.newadvent.org/cathen/06217a.htm (accessed March 16, 2020).

"Saint Anthony Chapel"https://saintanthonyschapel.org/ (accessed Feb 25, 2020).

"Saint Anthony of Padua,"Messaggero di S.Antonio Editrice, https://www.santantonio.org/en. (accessed March 8, 2020)

"Sé Cathedral Lisbon," https://lisbonlisboaportugal.com/ Alfama-Lisbon/se-cathedral-lisbon.html (accessed March 21, 2020).

"Secular Franciscan Order" https://secularfranciscansusa.org/ (accessed March 7, 2020).

"The Shrine of St. Anthony"http://ShrineofStAnthony.org. (accessed Feb 26, 2020).

"Sisters of St. Francis of the Providence of God,"https://www. osfprov.org/(accessed March 5, 2020),

"St. Anthony's Guild: Home" https://stanthonysguild.org/ (accessed March 9, 2020).

"St. Anthony School Programs," 2017, https://www. stanthonykids.org. (accessed Feb 8, 2020).

"St. Bonaventure"www.newadvent.org/cathen/02648c. htm(March 8, 2020).

"St. Francis Chapel" https://www.atonementfriars.org/ graymoor-holy-mountain/#st_francis_chapel. (accessed March 7, 2020).

"St. Louis de Montfort," http://www.newadvent.org/ cathen/09384a.htm (accessed March 4, 2020).

Jocelyn Thomas, "St. Anthony's Guild Plans 90th Anniversary Celebration," *Around the Province*.https://hnp.org/ communications/articles-and-speeches/. (accessed March 5, 2014).

"Unfailing Prayer to St. Anthony"https://www.catholic.org/prayers/prayer.php?=163 (accessed March 8, 2020).

"US Franciscans" https://usfranciscans.org (accessed March 5, 2020).

Jack Wintz. *Saint Francis and the Crib,* Franciscan Media, 2020, https://franciscanmedia.org/saint-francis-and-the-crib/. (accessed March 22, 2020).

Pictorial Index

LOST AND FOUND

Directions: Find out who owns these lost articles by reading Part II: Oral History Project.

ALEX AND ANI bracelets
Divinely-placed cellphone
diamond pendant
Duquesne University class ring
eye-catching diamond ring
international parcel
irreplaceable earring

man's wedding band
men's eyeglasses
priceless keys
Trader Joe's gift card
"twofer:" GPS and camera
wallet
women's eyeglasses

OTHER WORKS BY THIS AUTHOR:

A Sociological And Ethnomusicological Study
Of Billie Holiday And Her Music
(University of Pittsburgh, 1999)

ENDNOTES

1 Vergilio Gamboso, ed. Life of St Anthony: Assidua. Translated by Bernard Przewozny, (Padova: Messaggero, 2019), 5.

2 Gamboso, ed., "Here Begin the Miracles of Blessed Anthony" in Assidua, 67-95.

3 Michael E. Gaitley, 33 Days to Morning Glory, (Marian Press: Stockbridge Mass. 2015).

4 Michael E. Gaitley, Consoling the Heart of Jesus, (Lighthouse Catholic Media: Sycamore, Illinois, 2010.

5 Grzegorz Górny. Guadalupe Mysteries: deciphering the code, (Ignatius Press: San Francisco, 2016).

6 We Knew What We Had: The Greatest Jazz Story Never Told, YouTube video, 1:12. Posted by MCGJazz. Feb 2, 2018. https://www.youtube.com/watch?v=JUs5tovT7EQ (accessed March 25, 2020).

7 Singing in the Rain, Directed by Gene Kelly and Stanley Donen. Culver California: MGM, 1952.

8   Saint Augustine (of Hippo), The Confessions of S. Augustine, (J. Parker & Co.: London,1868).

9   Basilica Pontificia di Sant'Antonio di Padova (Basilica of Saint Anthony of Padua), is the site where the body of St. Anthony is entombed and his relics are venerated. In the days and weeks following Anthony's funeral, the number of miracles occurring at his tomb helped make a strong case for his canonization, and this took place less than a year after his death, June 13,1231. First entombed in his small friary, after the construction of a basilica encompassing that space, his tomb was moved, and it has been moved additional times over the years with various structural modifications and enhancements to the basilica. The breathtaking side altar was begun in 1500 and completed towards the end of that century. Via a live webcam at the site, St. Anthony's tomb can be viewed 24 hours a day. "Saint Anthony of Padua," Messaggero di S.Antonio Editrice, 2020, (March 8, 2020), https://www.santantonio.org/en. According to Maria Hart, the Director of the Anthonian Association in the U.S., this is a worldwide non-profit and charitable organization. The O.F.M. Conventuals of the basilica are responsible for the monthly publication, The Messenger of Saint Anthony which has worldwide distribution, now in 35 countries. Subscription to the magazine is available through the above website. Telephone conversation March 25, 2020.

10 Padre Giuseppe Abate (1889-1969) Franciscan friar. Gamboso, Life of Saint Anthony, 141

11 Gamboso, Life of Saint Anthony, 141-142.

12 Matt. 7:7-8 (NAB).

13 Saint Anthony Chapel, 1704 Harpster Street, Pittsburgh, Pa 15212, (412) 323-9504. Construction of the devotional chapel was completed in 1883, and the dedication of the chapel took place on June 13, Anthony's feast day. The annex was completed in 1892. The Thirteen Tuesday Novena in honor of St. Anthony of Padua is conducted every year, scheduled to conclude on June 13. The chapel contains over five thousand relics of saints, reputedly "the most venerated relic," a tooth of St. Anthony. The chapel has been designated a Historical Landmark by the Pittsburgh History and Landmarks Foundation. "Saint Anthony Chapel," e-Catholic, (accessed Feb 25, 2020), https://stanthonyschapel.org/the-chapel.

14

15 KofC contributed more than $185 million to charity and donated more than 76 million hours of service in the U.S. and abroad to mentioned programs as well as Coats for Kids, Christian Refugee Relief, and Disaster Relief. "Knights of Columbus," 2020, (accessed March 6, 2020), https://www.kofc.org/. According to Gary Williard, KofC member of St. Elizabeth Ann Seton Council #11143, the council is the joint effort of this community. Cards are sent to shut-ins, and they hold Bingo monthly for residents in nursing homes. They coordinate activities for Divine Mercy Sunday. Numerous team projects include manning festival booths and holding pancake breakfasts. Members sell lottery calendars and COAL tickets, and their annual Tootsie Roll Drive raises funds for the council and for local organizations such as St. Anthony School Programs and McGuire Home. The Baby Bottle Campaign is a local outreach to support mothers in need.

In support of life, the Rosary is prayed outside some places where abortions are likely to occur. Our local has vans fitted with ultrasound machines that save lives, "helping women choose life...giving them the opportunity to view their unborn children. Once the expectant mothers see their babies, over 80% carry their babies full term."

"Knights of Columbus," 2020, (accessed March 6, 2020), https://www.kofc.org/en/what-we-do/faith-in-action-programs/life/ultrasound-program.html

16 Matt. 7:21 and Matt. 25:31-46 (NAB).

17 Matt. 25:23 "Come, share your master's joy!"

18 St. Anthony School Programs serve a 4-county area, providing educational programs for children of all faiths who are challenged with Down Syndrome, Autism Spectrum Disorder and Intellectual Disabilities. Allegheny County site: 2000 Corporate Dr. #580, Wexford, Pa.15090, (844) 782-5437. In the South Hills, St. Thomas More Catholic School integrates the St. Anthony School Program into its student body for children ages K-8. "St. Anthony School Programs," 2017, (accessed Feb 8, 2020), https://www.stanthonykids.org/.

19 According to Father Jerome, The Guild of St. Anthony is a pious society, a lay organization. It was founded in Nigeria by missionary priests in 1920 as part of the modern Catholic mission, when various lay organizations emerged. The Guild of St. Anthony is not to be confused with St. Anthony's Guild, a fundraising organization guided by the Franciscan Friars. Holy Name Province, 144 West 32nd St., New York, NY 10001 (212) 564-8799. "St. Anthony's Guild: Home"

(accessed March 9, 2020), https://stanthonysguild.org/. St. Anthony's Guild was founded in the U.S. in 1924 by John Forrest Loviner, (Order of Friars Minor) who had been born on the feast day of St. Anthony of Padua in 1896 in Columbus, Ohio. A year after Loviner's ordination, working from the Bonaventure Friary in Paterson, New Jersey, he purchased a building there and in 1927 began publication of the Anthonian. The guild print shop, which opened in 1930, became one of the largest producers of catechetical literature in the U.S. (Figures 4 and 5 are samples). add corresponding page numbers of THIS book when available)

"John Forest Loviner" (accessed March 9, 2020), https://st.anthonysguild./hnp-friars/john-forest-loviner.

Jocelyn Thomas, "St. Anthony's Guild Plans 90th Anniversary Celebration," Around the Province, (accessed March 5, 2014), https://hnp.org/communications/articles-and-speeches/.

20 This beautiful story resembles a traditional Italian narrative recounted by Stoddard, Saint Anthony portrayed as a protector of children: The mother sees her child fall from a high window, and she cries to Anthony for help. As she rushes to her son, he runs to her and says, "A friar caught me in his arms and placed me gently on the ground." The mother then takes her child to offer thanks at Ara Coeli, the old Franciscan church in Rome. Upon entering the church, the little boy points to a picture and says, "See, there is the friar who saved me!" The pictured saint was Anthony of Padua.

Charles Warren Stoddard, "The Glories of Anthony" in Saint
Anthony: The Wonder-Worker of Padua, ed. (Charlotte,
N.C., TAN Books, 1978) 97-98.

21 The term Franciscan traces from St. Francis of Assisi
(b.1181/1182–October 3,1226)."Francis insolently
followed the early teaching of his parents right up to the
twenty-fifth year of his life, squandered his time vainly,
practice of vanities and revelry...One day the Lord revealed
to him in prayer what he needed to do...truly held riches in
contempt and despised money. He went among the lepers...
kissed them...and cleansing the pus from their sores...He
began to preach penance to everyone, granted in simple
words, but with a magnificent heart. He began by saying,
as the Lord had revealed to him, 'May the Lord give you
peace.'" Thomas of Celano. The Rediscovered Life of St.
Francis of Assisi, ed. Jacques Dalarun and trans. Timothy J.
Johnson (St. Bonaventure University: Franciscan Institute
Publications, 2016), 2-6.

"The foundation of the Poor Ladies or Second Order" of
Franciscans "may be said to have been laid in 1212. In that
year St. Clare who had besought St. Francis to be allowed
to embrace the new manner of life he had instituted, was
established by him at St. Damian's near Assisi, together
with several other pious maidens who had joined her."
Francis did not "draw up a formal rule for these Poor ladies
and no mention of such a document is found in any of the
early authorities. The rule imposed upon the Poor Ladies at
St. Damian's about 1219 by Cardinal Ugolino, afterwards
Gregory IX, was recast by St. Clare towards the end of her
life, with the assistance of Cardinal Rinaldo, afterwards
Alexander IV, and in this revised form was approved

by Innocent IV, 9 Aug., 1253 (Litt. "Solet Annuere")." "Franciscan Order" 2017, (accessed March 5, 2020), http://www.newadvent.org/cathen/06217a.htm.

The Poor Ladies' followers became known as the Poor Clares, and continue their mission today, as do many incarnations of this ideal. Locally, the Sisters of St. Francis of the Providence of God "have provided a child-centered environment for children for 35 years" at The Franciscan Child Day Care Center in Whitehall. Their mission, "Childcare is in our Hearts and Children are the Heart of our Center," is "inspired by Francis of Assisi to follow Jesus Christ in total responsiveness to the Providence of God...and to proclaim peace in the joy of the spirit." "Sisters of St. Francis of the Providence of God," 2020, (accessed March 5, 2020), www.franciscanchilddaycare.org.

22 This is the "Unfailing Prayer to St. Anthony." The prayer begins: "Blessed be God in His Angels and in His Saints." "Unfailing Prayer to St. Anthony" (accessed March 8, 2020) https://www.catholic.org/prayers/prayer.php?=163. The original prayer card was obtained from Franciscan Friars of the Atonement at Graymoor, 40 Franciscan Way, Garrison, NY, 10524. (888) 720-8247. Graymoor has acquired from Assisi the altar where St. Francis received his holy stigmata on Mt. Alverna in 1224, now located there in the St. Francis Chapel. According to Director of Communications Jonathon Hotz, there is a statue of St. Francis of Assisi above the altar which is one of only two made from a mold of Francis' death mask (the other is in Assisi). At the left side of the altar is a statue of St. Anthony, and this is where Father Paul Wattson, S.A. and the Friars began their perpetual novena to St. Anthony in 1912.

(accessed March 7, 2020), https://www.atonementfriars. org/graymoor-holy-mountain/#st_francis_chapel.

Anthony's true likeness can be seen on the front cover of Spilsbury's recent volume. The impressive "bust in bronze" by Roberto Cremesini, sculpted in 1995, was obtained through advanced techniques—"forensic reconstruction derived from the measurements of the Saint's skull performed during the 1981 examination." Paul Spilsbury, Saint Anthony of Padua: His Life and Writings, 2nd Reprint (P.P.F.M.C. Messaggero Di Sant'Antonio-Editrice 2015) front cover.

23 Secular Franciscans are also referred to as lay Franciscans, a branch of the Franciscan Family formed by lay Catholic men and women who seek to observe the Gospel of Jesus by following the example of St. Francis of Assisi. "Secular Franciscan Order–USA," 2020, (accessed March 7, 2020), secularfranciscansusa.org.

The Secular Franciscan Order (Ordo Franciscanus Saecularis), also known as the Third Order, was "founded by Francis about 1221 calls devout persons...living in the world and following a rule of life approved by Nicholas IV in 1289, and modified by Leo XIII, 30 May, 1883" (Constit. "Misericors"). "Franciscan Order" 2017, (accessed March 7, 2020), www.newadvent.org/cathen/06217a.htm.

24 The San Damiano (Saint Damian) cross is that cross before which Francis prayed in the Assisi church he would rebuild, early in his conversion. Bonaventure wrote a biography of Francis in 1263 which tells how this came about: "For one day when Francis went out to meditate in the fields, he walked near the church of San Damiano which was

threatening to collapse because of age. Impelled by the Spirit, he went inside to pray. Prostrate before an image of the Crucified, he was filled with no little consolation as he prayed. While his tear-filled eyes were gazing at the Lord's cross, he heard with his bodily ears a voice coming from that cross, telling him three times: "Francis, go and repair my house which, as you see, is all being destroyed."

Trembling, Francis was stunned at the sound of such an astonishing voice, since he was alone in the church; and as he absorbed the power of the divine words into his heart, he fell into an ecstasy of mind. At last, coming back to himself, he prepared himself to obey and pulled himself together to carry out the command of repairing the material church, although the principal intention of the words referred to that which Christ purchased with his own blood..."

"His Perfect Conversion to God and His Repair of 3 Churches," Regis Armstrong, Wayne Hellmann, and William J Short, eds. Vol.2, 1999-2001. Franciscan Intellectual Tradition.The Life of Blessed Francis: FA:ED, vol. 2, p. 536. (accessed March 23, 2020) https://www.franciscantradition. org/francis-of-assisi-early-documents/the-founder/the-legends-and-sermons-about-saint-francis-by-bonaventure-of-bagnoregio/the-major-legend-of-saint-francis/the-life-of-blessed-francis/1625-fa-ed-2-page-536#ges:sea rchword=san+damiano+cross&searchphrase=all&page=1.

The Tau cross is also of great significance. Tau is the upper-case form of the letter T in the Greek alphabet, and there is a reference in the Old Testament Book of Ezekiel to its use among penitents: "This conviction should be faithfully and devotedly in the forefront of our minds: not only does this advance the mission he held of calling to weep and mourn, {snippet Is 22:12} to shave one's head and wear sackcloth, and to sign the Tau {snippet Ez 9:4} on the foreheads of those moaning and grieving with a sign of a penitential cross, and of a habit conformed to the cross..."

Prologue, Regis Armstrong, O.F.M. Cap., Wayne Hellmann, O.F.M. Conv., and William J. Short., eds. Vol. 2,1999-2001. The Life of Blessed Francis: FA:ED, vol. 2, p. 527 (March 23,2020) https://www.franciscantradition.org/francis-of-assisi-early-documents/the-founder/the-legends-and-sermons-about-saint-francis-by-bonaventure-of-bagnoregio/the-major-legend-of-saint-francis/the-life-of-blessed-francis/1616-fa-ed-2-page-527#ges:searchword%3Dtau%2Bcross%26searchphrase%3Dall%26page%3D1.

"St. Francis used the Tau in his writings, and even used it as his signature."

"Friar's E-spirations:The Franciscan Coat of Arms" (accessed April 22,2020) https://www.franciscanmedia.org/friar-s-e-spirations-the-franciscan-coat-of-arms/.

25 The Shrine of St. Anthony, in Ellicott City, Maryland 21042, is a ministry of the Franciscan Friars Conventual, a branch of the order founded for men by Francis of Assisi in 1209. (accessed March 18, 2020) https://www.merriam-webster.com/dictionary/conventual. (accessed Feb 26, 2020) "The Shrine of St. Anthony" http://ShrineofStAnthony.org.

The Gospel life of the Friars Minor today has "four central components: 1. to be men of prayer, 2 .to live as lesser ones, 3. to create a brotherhood of mutual care among ourselves, and 4. to go about the world as heralds of God's reign and agents of Gospel peace." "USFranciscans" accessed March 5, 2020.accessed March 5, 2020. https://usfranciscans.org.

In our modern world, these charisms translate to the 3 branches of the First order, each containing all 4 components but with varied focus. One way of looking at the differences is the way the Conventuals live in a "convent," in brotherhood and community; Capuchins in prayer and contemplation with greater solitude; and Friars Minor make up a larger population, seeking involvement in the apostolate of active ministry.

Biographers of Anthony have provided many examples of how he fulfilled his ministry with holiness and excellence in each area. Sophronius Clasen, for instance, makes the point that, "in a happy balance of the apostolate and the life of solitude, he surrendered himself after the example of saints to the all-wise guidance of God.

Sophronius Clasen, St. Anthony: Doctor of the Church, translated by Ignatius Brady, (Franciscan Herald Press: Chicago 1973), 63.

Vergilio Gamboso describes Anthony's standing in the Order just after Francis' death:

"At the Chapter meeting of 1227, Anthony had already "made a well-deserved name for himself in propagating the Order in France and was highly respected for his intellectual gifts and holy lifestyle. He was chosen as Provincial Minister of Emilia, a vast, densely populated area in Northern Italy...and embroiled in heresy and conflict." He "governed his friars with clemency and kindness. He seemed less a Superior than a comrade," and "remained admirably courteous," even though "he surpassed all men in Italy for eloquence and doctrinal knowledge." Gamboso, Life of Saint Anthony, 90-91.

26 Sacro Convento di San Francesco d'Assisi (Sacred Convent of Saint Francis) is a Franciscan friary where the mortal remains of St. Francis and those of his first companions have been resting in the basilica. The friars have custody of the body of St. Francis. The website provides a live webcam for 24-hour visitation to the crypt. Basilica di San Francesco d'Assisi (accessed March 9, 2020) https://www.sanfrancescoassisi.org.

27 Companions of St. Anthony is a mission for the advancement and development of the Franciscan friars of the province, The Holy Name Province. Primarily the funds are for their education and for support of the Shrine of St. Anthony in Ellicott City, Md. "Companions of St. Anthony" (accessed Feb 18, 2020), https//www.companionsofstanthony.org.

28 Holy Land Treasures USA offers hand-carved olivewood creations. According to the information on the website, many of the olive trees are supplied from the Galilee region, the wood carved by a local artisan at their factory on Manger Street in Bethlehem, Palestine. The finished piece comes with a certificate of authenticity, "Made in the Holy Land." In the U.S., their gift shop is located in Wake County, North Carolina. "Holy Land Treasures" (accessed Feb 18, 2020) https://www.holylandtreasuresonline.com.

29 Saint Louis-Marie Grignion de Montfort (1673-1716), was a French priest and Confessor as well as an early writer in the field of Mariology. Known in his time for his devotion

to the Blessed Virgin Mary and the practice of saying the Rosary, he was a charismatic preacher who combated heresy and ministered to soldiers. There is a story from La Rochelle, France of him ministering to "soldiers who were so moved by his words, they wept and cried for the forgiveness of their sins. In the procession which terminated this mission, an officer walked at the head, barefooted and carrying a banner, and the soldiers also barefooted, carrying in one hand a crucifix, in the other a rosary, and singing hymns."(accessed March 4, 2020) "St. Louis de Montfort," http://www.newadvent.org/cathen/09384a.htm.

30 Eternal Word Television Network is an American-based cable television network that broadcasts round-the-clock Catholic themed programming. It was founded in 1981 by Mother Mary Angelica (b.1923, Canton, Ohio, d. 2016, Hanceville, Alabama), a member of the cloistered nuns, the Poor Clares. (March 11, 2020) https://www.ewtn.com.

The EWTN staff of Franciscan friars "come from around the country and around the world." Some familiar faces to the television audience include Fr. Joseph Mary, Fr. Mark Mary, Fr. John Paul Mary, and Br. John Therese Marie. "The Friars" (March 11, 2020) https://franciscanmissionaries. com/the-friars/.

The upbeat ICONS features young twin Franciscan Friars of the Renewal, Fr. Innocent Montgomery and Fr. Angelus Montgomery as well as Fr. Augustino Torres. "Icons," (accessed March 11, 2020) https://www.ewtn.com/tv/ shows/icons.

31 According to parishioner Rajkumar Manoharan who is a native of Chennai, Tamilnadu, India, the indigenous

Thamizh (Tamil) dialect spoken in this southern region has multiple pronunciations for the British English digraph /th/. So that spelling may be pronounced either AN-tho-nee or AN-to-nee

32   (Luke 18: 1-8) NAB

33   St. Bonaventure (1221-1274) was born in Italy during the time of Francis of Assisi, and the traditional story is that he received this name as a result of an exclamation of Francis when the child's mother pleaded with him to pray for her little son who was very ill. Francis' gifts allowed him to foresee a great future for this child, and so Francis exclaimed, "O buona ventura!" (O good fortune) Indeed the boy would grow up healthy, and when he was twenty-two he entered the Franciscan Order. "St. Bonaventure" (March 8, 2020), http://www.newadvent.org/cathen/02648c.htm.

"In 1263, the new Basilica of St. Anthony was completed, and his remains were re-interred in a more magnificent tomb on the Octave of Easter."By this time, Bonaventure was Minister General of the Franciscans, and so he presided. When the Saint's remains were disinterred, it was found that his tongue was incorrupt, as red and soft as it had been thirty and more years before. St. Bonaventure took it into his hands and venerated it: "O blessed tongue which ever blessed the Lord and made others bless him! Now it is abundantly clear how much you merited from God." "This event was widely reported, and gave fresh impetus to the Anthonian cultus." Paul Spilsbury, Saint Anthony of Padua: His Life and Writings, 2nd Reprint (Messaggero Di Sant'Antonio-Editrice 2015)140.

34 St. Vincent de Paul Society was founded in Paris in 1833 to help the people living in slums. Today the organization is a registered non-profit whose lay Catholic members, called "Vincentians," seek personal holiness through works of charity. The society's mission is to live the gospel message by serving Christ in the poor with love, respect, hope, and joy, and by working to shape a more just and compassionate society. They accept donations for the operation of several thrift stores and food banks to benefit the poor and needy. Our Catholic community helpline is (412) 444-5425. "Society of St. Vincent De Paul" (accessed March 8, 2020) http://svdppitt.org.

35 St. Anthony Mission Partner-My Mass Request-Seraphic Mass Association & Capuchin Mission Office, 5217 Butler Street, suite 100, Pittsburgh Pa, 15201. (877)737-9050. (accessed March 10, 2020) "Become a St. Anthony Mission Partner," https://mymassrequest.org/Ways-to-Give/ St-Anthony-Mission-Partners/Join

36 Basilica of the National Shrine of Mary, Queen of the Universe is at 8300 Vineland Ave., Orlando, Florida. 32821. Construction began on December 8, 1984. The construction of the massive, expertly crafted pipe organ consisting of 5,271 pipes, will be completed in November, 2020. "Basilica of the National Shrine of Mary, Queen of the Universe," (accessed March 12, 2020) https://www. maryqueenoftheuniverse.org.

When Saint Anthony was to be baptized "Fernando" in Lisbon, Portugal, his parents had only to walk across the street from their home to Sé, the grand, new Romanesque cathedral named Santa Maria Maior de Lisboa (St. Mary

Major of Lisbon). Fernando attended school there, and, by all accounts, he was devoted to Mary throughout his life.

Sophronius Clasen, St. Anthony: Doctor of the Church, trans. Ignatius Brady,(Franciscan Herald Press: Chicago 1973) 4-7.

On November 1,1755, an earthquake, by today's estimates from 8.5–9 on the moment magnitude scale and a tsunami, destroyed most of Lisbon killing 60,000 people. The cathedral survived however, and extensive repairs, renovations, and modifications have been carried out through the centuries, its upper story now an exhibition of liturgical, devotional and catechism items. Mass is celebrated in the sanctuary.

"Lisbon earthquake of 1755," accessed March 21, 2020) https://www.britannica.com/even/Lisbon-earthquake-of-1755. "Sé Cathedral Lisbon," (accessed March 21, 2020) https://lisbonlisboaportugal.com/Alfama-Lisbon/se-cathedral-lisbon.html.

37 Luke 1:30-32

38 Thomas of Celano, 25.

39 Michael P. Warsaw, Christmas '19 Family Newsletter, EWTN Global Catholic Network, Christmas 2019, cover.

40 "Today in Greccio, one can still see the stone—perhaps three feet high and two feet wide—on which the hay was placed...The top has a rough, shallow, V-shaped indentation. Here the carved image of the baby was laid." Jack Wintz, "Saint Francis and the Crib,"Franciscan Media,

2020, (accessed March 22, 2020) https://franciscanmedia. org/saint-francis-and-the-crib/.

41 Jack Wintz, Saint Anthony of Padua: His Life, Legends, and Devotions,(St. Anthony Messenger Press, U.S., 2012), 40-41.

42 Gamboso, ed., Assidua, 89-91.

CPSIA information can be obtained
at www.ICGtesting.com
Printed in the USA
BVHW020527260322
632492BV00002B/2

9 781631 294457